Caught in a Tornado

A
Chinese American
Woman
Survives the
Cultural
Revolution

Caught in a Tornado

James R. Ross

Northeastern University Press
Boston

Northeastern University Press

Library of Congress Cataloging-in-Publication Data
Ross, James R. (James Rodman), 1950–
    Caught in a tornado: A Chinese American woman survives
the Cultural Revolution / James R. Ross.
        p. cm.
    Includes bibliographical references and index.
    ISBN 1-55553-192-X
    1. Wen Zengde, 1900– 2. Chinese American women—
Biography. 3. China—History—Cultural Revolution, 1966–1969.
I. Title
E184.C5R67   1994
951.05—dc20   94-5621

Designed by Milenda Nan Ok Lee

Composed in Sabon by Coghill Composition, Richmond,
Virginia. Printed and bound by Thomson-Shore, Inc., Dexter,
Michigan. The paper is Supple Opaque Recycled, an acid-
free stock.

MANUFACTURED IN THE UNITED STATES OF AMERICA
98 97 96 95 94   5 4 3 2 1

In Memory of Wen Zengde

Contents

Contents

Acknowledgments

It took more than eight years to research, write, and rewrite this book. In its earliest drafts, my friend Paul Wilkes coached me through my tentative first steps in learning—after fifteen years as a journalist—to become a writer. He also recommended me to his agent, Alison Bond. Alison agreed to represent me and continued to believe in this story through its many rewritings. I owe my greatest debt to John Weingartner, senior editor at Northeastern University Press, who was captivated by Wen's story and skillfully supervised its final revisions and publication.

A number of former teachers and students from the Shanghai Foreign Languages Institute (now Shanghai International Studies University) generously assisted me in reporting this story, particularly Guan Keguang and Shi Songchuan. Wen Zengde's son, Daniel Chen, offered useful suggestions and helped me reproduce some of the pictures that appear in this book. I also thank the University of Pittsburgh and the University of Connecticut for faculty research grants in support of my work and the University of Pittsburgh Contempo-

Acknowledgments

rary China Program for funding my travels to China to teach and do research.

My wife, Irene Coletsos, read and commented on the numerous revisions of this manuscript and encouraged me to continue when I was certain the manuscript would never make it into print. Her support, and Wen's spirit, made this book possible.

Author's Note

I first met Wen Zengde in July 1987 at her modest apartment in Oakland, California. She lived near the city's Chinatown, in a housing complex for the elderly not far from the YMCA. Wen greeted me as I walked off the elevator across from her apartment, and I was surprised at how frail and tiny she seemed. Her face was weathered and her hair mostly gray, but she seemed energetic for age eighty-seven. (Wen was the youngster in her family. Her eldest sister, aged 102, lived only a few miles away and, Wen confided, was "beginning to act old.") Wen dressed simply, in a print housedress. Her apartment was simple, too, decorated with family photographs, including one remarkable picture of Wen aboard a parade float in San Francisco in 1912 celebrating the overthrow of China's monarchy.

Wen's mind was still quick and her endurance seemed boundless. She had prepared well for my visit in the time since I had written her in May and asked for an interview. When I arrived, she handed me a ninety-one-page handwritten account of her ten years in China during the Cultural

Revolution, "A Recollection of How I Was Caught in a Tornado."

Wen had been a teacher at the Shanghai Foreign Languages Institute, where I had taught journalism in the summers of 1985 and 1986. I had traveled throughout China during those two summers and, as someone who was new to the country, was fascinated and horrified by the stories I heard from survivors of the Cultural Revolution. I interviewed a number of teachers from the Foreign Languages Institute and hoped to write an account of their experiences. (An earlier book, Neale Hunter's *Shanghai Journal*, had provided a rather sanitized portrayal of the Cultural Revolution at the school and in Shanghai.) In 1986–87, I traveled to Europe and around the United States interviewing former Foreign Languages Institute teachers who were living abroad. They led me to Wen.

She and I met every day for a week during July 1987, starting our interviews at 7 A.M. and continuing through dinner. I soon realized that her story was far more than an account of the Cultural Revolution. Wen told me about growing up in a Chinese immigrant family in San Francisco at the turn of the century; meeting with Sun Yatsen when he stayed at her family's home on a fund-raising trip to the United States; and traveling to China for the first time as a teenager to attend college there. She also talked about her marriage to a general and government official who introduced her to Chinese high society and her family's escape from the Japanese invaders in 1941 and flight to the Chinese countryside. She recalled how the Communists had invited her to return to China from Hong Kong in 1955 and teach English in Shanghai. It was ten years later, when Wen was well into her sixties, that she became a victim of the Cultural Revolution. (At times, overwhelmed by my persistent questioning, Wen jokingly compared me to the Red Guards who had brutally interrogated her twenty years earlier.)

We exchanged lengthy letters for more than a year after those first sessions and met again for another week of interviews the following summer. As I continued to study Chinese history and culture, I began to understand Wen's viewpoint. She saw China through a prism of both American and Chinese values, an unusual perspective not only on the Cultural Revolution but also on much of twentieth-century China.

At first, it was easy for me to see Wen as a victim, a woman unjustly persecuted by irrational tormentors. She suffered greatly during those ten years, as did dozens of others at the Foreign Languages Institute and millions throughout China. But I also began to understand that the Cultural Revolution was not an isolated event and was far more complicated than a battle of good against evil.

Wen's life was caught up in the eternal conflict in Chinese society between respect for foreign ideas and the danger of being controlled by them. Her American upbringing gave Wen a sense of justice that helped her survive, yet it also led many Chinese to distrust her because of their antagonism toward the United States. Wen enjoyed relative wealth and privilege during her years in China, but her status also sharply separated her from her students and colleagues who came from less-privileged families.

The issues Wen faced in her lifetime have not yet been resolved. In fact, as China hurtles toward capitalism and overcomes the legacy of the Cultural Revolution, it may be further than ever from facing the conflicts of corruption, class inequality, and foreign influence that have divided the nation for centuries.

Caught in a Tornado

Prologue
(November 1966)

It was nearly 1:30 A.M. but Wen Zengde was still awake. Her housemaid had stayed late that night, and the two of them were up talking, anticipating another visit from the Red Guards. The Guards had been roaming their neighborhood for weeks now, storming into houses and apartments to ask for food and confiscating money and jewelry. A loud knock on the door of her second-floor apartment interrupted their conversation.

Wen walked to the balcony and opened the door halfway. She could make out only one figure, wearing a Red Guard armband, outside in the darkness. Wen didn't recognize him.

"What do you want?" she asked harshly.

"Let me inside," the young man said. "Then I will tell you."

It was the fourth time the Red Guards had been to Wen's apartment this month and she was losing patience. The first search was an official one, and the Guards were accompanied by young teachers, Wen's colleagues at the Shanghai Foreign Languages Institute. They had opened her closets, bureau drawers, trunks, and suitcases, searching for goods that represented the "four olds"—old ideas, old customs, old culture, and old habits—that Mao Zedong had instructed them to destroy. When they left, they took her woolen overcoats, some dresses, silverware, carved ivory frames, and some antiques. Wen was relieved that they hadn't found her American passport, which she had wrapped in cellophane and buried in a flowerpot on her balcony.

Two nights later, a group of six or seven Red Guards had come at midnight, asking to see "the bourgeois ideologist Wen Zengde." Wen didn't recognize any of them, but they spoke with Beijing accents. Two of them pushed her out on the balcony while the others began ransacking the room. Wen watched through the balcony window as one grabbed a letter opener, knife, and pair of scissors and hid them in his pocket. Others took Wen's valuable Chinese art: a Tang dynasty scroll, a Qing dynasty painting of the goddess of mercy, and a fan that had been hand-painted by a famous opera singer. They also stole writing brushes, ink blocks, and even Wen's jade chop, the stamp she used to sign her name. The Guards stuffed all their booty into one of Wen's suitcases, let her back in the house, and left.

Yesterday, a third group of Red Guards had been to Wen's apartment, again sometime around midnight. Wen had woken up to hear some kicking at her door. She found six Red Guards there, all students from the Spanish department. They asked for something to eat, and Wen found them some food and wine. After their meal, the Guards began searching.

One of them discovered a small box of jewelry in a trunk and scolded Wen for hiding it. He said he would turn it in to the revolutionary committee. But after the girls in the group looked inside the box, the jewelry quickly vanished. One took a pair of jade earrings, another grabbed a butterfly brooch and a pearl necklace. Then one of the girls noticed the Rolex watch on Wen's wrist and demanded it, too, but Wen convinced her she needed it to show up on time for meetings held on campus to criticize teachers and officials. The Red Guards had completed their search by closing up all the trunks and bookcases and sealing off Wen's study with two long, narrow strips of paper that formed an X. They signed and dated the seal, imitating the ancient tradition of high government authorities who searched houses of people under suspicion.[1]

Wen had tried to remain calm during all these visits. But she was afraid of what the Red Guards might do next and had asked her maid, Shen Bixia, to stay with her tonight after Shen cooked dinner. Wen felt more secure with Shen there, and she was ready to lecture this arrogant young man who had knocked at her door one and a half hours after midnight and disturbed her peace. He spoke before she had a chance to begin; he was not there to search the apartment.

"You are to come with me to the Foreign Languages Institute right away," he said. "You must bring your treasured red book [of Mao's quotations], a mosquito net, a straw mat, a hand basin, a bowl, a pair of chopsticks, a mug, toothbrush, towel, and an extra set of clothes."

It was a list of goods for an inmate. Wen knew she was about to lose her freedom.

Shen started to cry as she helped Wen pack her things. Then she picked up the suitcase and told the Red Guard she would accompany him and Wen. But the Red Guard refused. No one was to know where Wen would be kept.

"She is an old woman," Shen pleaded. "The bag is heavy and it is dark outside."

The Red Guard agreed to let Shen bring the suitcase as far as the school gate. The three of them walked there silently. At the gate, Wen forced a smile and said goodbye to her maid. The Red Guard led her across the campus to the women's dormitory, showed her inside a dark, empty room, and locked the door. Wen Zengde was now a prisoner of the Cultural Revolution.

In the darkness, a hundred memories and fears circled in Wen's mind. She thought of her husband's warning, when she left Hong Kong more than a decade earlier, that his background as an anti-Communist would cause trouble for her. She worried about her son, who had been labeled a rightist and sent recently to a labor camp somewhere in China. Wen remembered the screams she heard from the interrogation rooms at school after the Cultural Revolution had begun and her young colleague Song Yongqing's suicide. She thought of the Jews who had been persecuted and murdered in Nazi Germany. Was this to be the end of her life?

But one idea kept returning to her. She had committed no crimes. She always had been loyal to China, a teacher who had volunteered to serve the country's new leaders.

For the next ten years, Wen Zengde would suffer imprisonment, beatings, and forced labor on the school grounds and in the countryside. Many of her colleagues who faced similar hardships would not survive. Yet Wen, sixty-six years old when the Cultural Revolution began, endured. Unlike her colleagues, she could not be swayed by pressures from friends, neighbors, students, and fellow teachers. She never lost her faith in justice and her belief that she would be exonerated. That independence and sense of justice came from Wen's upbringing in the United States.

ONE
San Francisco
(1910)

 Sun Yatsen, who had been visiting the United States early in 1910 to raise money for China's revolution, was now busy teaching a ten-year-old girl how to make coffee. In private, Sun was quiet and studious. He had said nothing the morning before when Wen Zengde dutifully poured him coffee from a pot in which she had rapidly boiled two tablespoons of grounds for fifteen minutes. But on this day he intercepted her before she reached the kitchen. He patiently showed her how to make coffee, never hinting that yesterday's brew was the worst he'd ever drunk.

Sun, the future president of China, had been staying at the Wen family house on Clay Street for two days. His visit was a mysterious adventure for Wen Zengde, who had first met Sun five days ago in the St. Francis Hotel.

When he arrived in San Francisco, Sun took a suite in the hotel, but he felt his accommodations were too extravagant and he was too visible. He had been kidnapped by agents of the Qing government in 1896 and was constantly worried about his safety. Two of Sun's followers suggested they could move him to a private home at 914 Clay Street, where Wen Xingfei's family lived. Wen Xingfei was one of Sun's loyal supporters and now was working as editor in chief of *Sun Bao,* a pro-Sun newspaper in Honolulu. The house on Clay Street seemed safe—only Wen Xingfei's mother and four sisters lived there. But Sun's aides had been told that the youngest sister, Wen Zengde, was a mischievous tomboy.

Sun's followers, Wang Boyue and Lei Shinan, had come to the house to meet the Wen family and talk to Wen Zengde. Wang showed the young girl a magazine and pointed to a photograph. Did she know this man? She quickly identified him as Dr. Sun Yatsen. Wang told her they would like her to meet Doctor Sun, but she had to be on her best behavior and greet him with respect. Then they took her to his luxurious hotel suite. The moment they opened the door and she saw Sun, Wen yelled out her greeting.

"Hello, teacher," Wen said, using the respectful form of address. "I am Little Eight."

Little Eight was her nickname—she was the youngest in a family of eight children. Sun welcomed her, took her hand, and asked about her older brother. He also asked about her family and their home and seemed satisfied that it would be a safe place to stay.

After the visit, Wang took Wen home and helped her family prepare the house. Sun would use the back door, Wang said, and he changed the locks and helped clear the hallway. Anyone who came to visit Sun would ring the back door buzzer three times—one long ring and two short ones.

Wen's mother and one of Wen's sisters moved out of their large bedroom, emptied their closets, and set up a desk for Sun. Wang told the family that they could have no visitors while Sun was there and asked them to keep a constant watch at the front window, looking out for anyone who lingered in the street or wore sunglasses. Wang also instructed Wen not to talk too much or ask Sun questions.

Sun spent most of his days writing. Wen's job was to make his bed, fix his bath, and bring him his meals. But Wen was too bold to simply perform chores.

On the second evening of Sun's stay, Wen approached him as he rested in a rocking chair in the sitting room.

"Teacher," she said, "why do you not shave off your mustache? You would look so much better without it." To Wen, a mustache seemed strange on a Chinese man. (Sun first grew a mustache as a disguise fifteen years earlier when he was being hunted for plotting to seize government offices in Canton.)[1]

Sun, who until then had seemed so serious, laughed loudly. Emboldened by his laughter, Wen asked more questions. She had heard about the revolution from her brother and wanted to know more. How was it that they could bring guns into China to help overthrow the monarchy? Sun was impressed by her knowledge and told her a story about smuggling weapons inside coffins across the border.

Sun left the next morning and didn't come back for three days. By the time he returned, Wen was ready with many more questions, and Sun seemed willing to talk with her for hours.

That evening, Sun told Wen the story of the British opium trade. He explained that the corrupt Manchu dynasty had exploited the farmers and workers and added to the wealth of the upper classes. Opium was illegal, but imports grew rapidly in the early 1800s as shippers bribed officials at China's borders and paid tributes to the monarchy. By the mid-1830s, Sun told her, the drug not only had addicted many bureaucrats and military officials but also was rapidly draining China's treasury. The government fought back when Britain demanded diplomatic recognition and equal trade, but its navy was no match for the British fleet in the Opium War. After its humiliating defeat, Sun said, the monarchy capitulated to the foreigners. The government remained weak, he said, and continued to survive only through foreign support.

Sun talked until the early hours of the morning. He was surprised that Wen had stories of her own to tell, including the tale of how she had helped raid a brothel to free some prostitutes. Among the alleys and passageways in the twelve square blocks of Chinatown, there were dozens of brothels and opium dens and hundreds of prostitutes on the streets.

Many of the women were the daughters of poor Chinese farmers. Some had been bought by Chinese merchants who promised to find them husbands in America. The merchants often forged their papers, paid for their second-class steamer tickets (first- and second-class passengers were not checked carefully by immigration officials), and then sold them to the brothels in Chinatown. These importers earned as much as two to three thousand dollars for each woman.[2]

The year before Sun's visit, Wen recalled proudly, she and two of her schoolmates, inspired by her older brother's discussions, had sneaked into the Long Feng brothel on Commercial Street. They smashed out the electric lights and led seven prostitutes four blocks to Donaldina Cameron's Chinese Presbyterian Mission at 900 Sacramento Street, a refuge for Chinese prostitutes since 1874.[3]

"You did the right thing," Sun said, explaining that Chinese families impoverished by opium addiction often sold their daughters to the traders. "That was a patriotic act."

Sun left early the next morning to continue his fund-raising tour. But he had won another follower. Wen soon was telling her classmates at the Oriental Public School about opium and how foreigners and a corrupt dynasty had made China weak. She asked them to help her support Sun.

A few weeks after Sun's visit, Wen organized what she called Sell Flowers Day to raise money. She visited the local florists and lectured them about Sun and the revolution, convincing them to donate boutonnieres and corsages. Then Wen and her classmates posted themselves at street corners and cable car stops, pinning the flowers on the suits and dresses of passersby. The students wore tin cans around their necks with a handwritten message: "Please help overthrow the Manchu dynasty. No change! Thank you."

Wen covered the area from Chinatown to Market Street, chasing down bankers in the business district. Although she was short, she managed to pin the flowers on their lapels before they could object. She asked for ten cents, but, like her classmates, didn't give change to anyone who might have only a quarter or a dollar coin. She raised more than two hundred dollars, and Sun's followers later presented her with an award.

That summer, Wen and her classmates decided they wanted to do more than raise money. They planned a raid on an opium den on Washington Street that was included on tours for visitors to Chinatown.

Her talk with Sun had convinced Wen that opium was a symbol of China's corruption and domination by foreigners. The den on Washington Street was even more humiliating— visitors went there to gawk at old men smoking opium pipes and women who showed them their bound feet.

One Saturday, Wen and two of her classmates cut into a line of tourists entering the den. Wen was the first one inside. She saw an old man wearing a long silk gown lying on a couch smoking an opium pipe. On the other side of the room was a middle-aged woman, her face covered with white makeup, sitting on a silk-covered bench and slowly untying the white cloth that bound her tiny, broken feet.

Wen was furious at what she saw. She ran across the room

and grabbed the bamboo pipe from the opium smoker, broke it in two, and threw it at him. Her classmates followed her example. As the tourists scattered, one of Wen's schoolmates smashed an oil lamp and the other picked up an urn of cooked opium and poured it on the floor. The woman with the bound feet hobbled out of the den, leaving a trail of white cloth behind her.

As the students prepared to leave, Wen saw a young girl in an embroidered silk gown, who served as a hostess for the den, trembling in a corner of the room. Wen recognized her as another of her classmates at the Oriental Public School.

"Do not be frightened," Wen told her. "We are not going to make more trouble for you. But this is to remind you how opium has made China poor and weak."

In some ways, Wen's youthful daring was similar to the Red Guards' attacks half a century later. Both the Red Guards and Wen struck at old habits and customs; they both were driven by nationalism, a belief that the old ways were obstacles to a strong and democratic China; and both of their causes led to revolutions that left China in turmoil.

But as a girl, Wen's dream seemed simple. She longed to live in a place where she could be proud to be Chinese. She had not found it in the United States. Sun Yatsen had been inspired by the principles of American democracy, and Wen had learned from him to value the American ideals of justice and equality. Yet she also understood that for Chinese and other minorities in the United States the ideal was masked by prejudice. Dozens of laws discriminated against the Chinese; for example, Wen was effectively barred from attending public schools in California.[4] Little had changed since her father and thousands of other Chinese had emigrated to California in search of fortune.

* * *

The first Chinese immigrants had arrived in California in 1848. More than 90 percent of those who followed were men—only merchants, students, and government officials could bring their wives and daughters with them. The immigrants worked as servants and cooks, mostly for Chinese businessmen involved in the fur trade between Canton and the West. But when word of the California gold rush reached China, thousands of men began to arrive from southern Chinese ports. Most made the seven-thousand-mile journey in crowded junks, with the same hopes for quick riches that captivated European immigrants arriving from the other side of the world. From the beginning, however, the Chinese were at the bottom of the ethnic ladder. They were driven away from profitable mines and could only work claims that others had abandoned.[5]

Outside of the gold fields, the Chinese always seemed to have the dirtiest jobs and the lowest pay. The exploitation of coolies, who laid almost seven hundred miles of track through the treacherous Sierra Nevada in the 1860s, was nearly synonymous with the digging and tunneling that built railroads in the West. As work on the railroad came to an end, the Chinese began to compete with other immigrants for jobs in agriculture and industry, and anti-Chinese discrimination began in earnest.

By the time the transcontinental railroad was completed in 1869, Chinese in California were refused admission to county hospitals, subject to special taxes, and effectively barred from public schools. They could not become citizens, testify in court, or marry a white person. The Chinese were driven from many occupations, yet they still found work by taking the least desirable jobs in canneries and in garment, broom, and cigar factories.[6]

The hostility toward the Chinese occasionally turned into violence. In 1871, a mob in Los Angeles hanged twenty

Chinese from a gallows. A few years later, immigrant European workers, blaming the Chinese for their low wages and lack of jobs, tried to burn down San Francisco's Chinatown.[7]

Emigration from China was virtually halted after 1882 by a federal law prohibiting any more Chinese from entering the country. By 1890, many Chinese had begun returning to the homeland. Between 1890 and 1900, the Chinese population of San Francisco—which had peaked at about thirty thousand people—dropped by 50 percent.[8]

Wen Zengde's father, Wen Wo, was one of the thousands of young Chinese who migrated to California in the 1860s. He was born in 1836, the second son of a landlord and scholar from Taishan, Guangdong Province. His father had died when Wen Wo was a young boy, and his family struggled to pay the increasing taxes levied by the government. In 1864, at the age of twenty-eight, Wen Wo decided to leave China for the United States. He sold some of the family land and mortgaged their store and house to raise money for the voyage, then sailed on a sixty-foot junk across the Pacific. It took three months to reach San Francisco.

Wen Wo was greeted by an association of fellow immigrants from Taishan and was introduced to people from families in his home town. The association invited him to help establish a school for their children, but Wen Wo declined. He had come to America to make his fortune.

Wen joined a group of Chinese immigrants and three young Americans who worked their way north looking for gold. They began digging in abandoned mines northeast of Sacramento, not far from where James Marshall had discovered gold in 1848 and set off the California gold rush. They worked there for a year with some success, then moved west to pan gold on the Feather River. The Chinese could work only at abandoned claims, but their diligence produced many ounces of gold. The group continued to take over abandoned claims in the Sierras, then moved west to the Trinity Mountains, and worked their way north until they reached Oregon three years later.

The modest success of some of the Chinese immigrants like Wen Wo spurred hate and resentment. As he traveled, Wen saw evidence of the growing discrimination against the Chinese. Chinese Must Go! banners were hung across the streets in small towns, and Wen met Chinese who had been driven out of their homes. He heard stories about others who were burned alive in their houses. Wen thought about returning home, as many Chinese immigrants were then doing.

But when they reached Portland, Oregon, in 1868, Jake Hoyt, one of the three Americans with whom Wen had been working, made plans to set up a lumber business. The company would buy timber in Oregon and transport it south to California, where there was a demand for wood to build houses. Wen and four of the other young Chinese miners decided to join him.

They called the business Wo Kee Lumber and Timber. Jake, Wen, and the four young Chinese bought timber in Portland and hauled it by horse-drawn cart to a Chinese-owned lumberyard in San Francisco. The day he joined the business, Wen bought a suit and tie—and a felt hat to cover his long braid of hair—then threw away his Chinese clothes.

Each trip by cart took nearly a month. In San Francisco, they paid the yard to saw and plane the wood, then sold the lumber to building contractors and the scrap to residents of Chinatown as firewood. On the return trip, the six of them hauled provisions to sell to the Chinese community in Portland, including dried shrimp, abalone, cuttlefish, Chinese sausages, and preserved eggs. Before the Chinese New Year, they brought joss sticks and colored paper. The business flourished and they traveled almost constantly between the two cities. Wen sent most of his savings to his mother in Taishan; she built two houses and acquired a large farm with his profits.

In 1878, after ten years in business, Wen decided to return to China to get married and to take care of his mother. He also was worried about his older brother—recent immigrants from his home town had told Wen that his brother was addicted to opium. Wen's mother arranged a match with a young woman from Taishan, Wong Hou, and Wen sailed back to China to marry her.

After the wedding, Wen confronted his older brother and demanded that he quit smoking opium. But it soon became clear his brother could not overcome his addiction. Wen Wo had hoped to stay in China, but he could not tolerate living with his brother. In 1881, he returned to San Francisco with his wife to rejoin his lumber business and raise a family. They lived near the lumber company's office on Pacific Street.

Their first child, a boy named Wen Xingfei, was born in 1885. When the boy was three, his father sent for a tutor from China to teach him Chinese. There was soon a house full of pupils. Wong Hou bore eight children, six girls and two boys. One boy and one girl died as infants. The youngest girl was born on August 6, 1900. Her Chinese name was Wen Zengde and her American birth certificate identified her as King G. Won. Her family called her Xiao Ba, "little eight."

Wen Wo continued to travel back and forth to Oregon but would stay for a few days with his family when he returned. He also enjoyed riding his pet white horse when he was at home. In October 1901, a few months after his youngest daughter's first birthday, Wen Wo spent a rainy afternoon riding. Late that afternoon, the horse came to the front door of the Wens' home, neighing wildly. Wong Hou thought her husband had returned from riding and filled a gunny sack with wheat and carrots to feed the horse. But he turned his head away and refused to eat. Instead, the horse led her to a field where Wen Wo had fallen. His hip was broken and he was sprawled on the ground, moaning in pain.

Wong Hou gently lifted her husband onto the horse and took him home. For twenty days, the family and a Chinese doctor treated him with traditional Chinese medicine. But he never recovered. The day he died, Wen Wo summoned his business partners and his family and divided his assets. He asked his only son to take care of his mother and sisters and told his wife to make sure all of the children received a good education. He closed his eyes and died peacefully.

Although Wen Zengde grew up without a father, she was always surrounded by siblings, friends, and relatives. And her neighborhood was rich with mystery and adventure, a place where the smells of fish, sandalwood incense, Chinese medicinal herbs, barbecued meat, and opium smoke mixed in the air.

In Wen's Chinatown, flowered lanterns hung in front of nearly every store and laundry covered carved wooden balconies. Shop windows displayed silk from Suzhou and tea-colored crystal from Jiangxi Province; food markets hung ducks and hams outside. There were Buddhist temples, theaters that produced Chinese plays, and three-story dim-sum restaurants where Wen would eat for hours with her mother and her mother's friends. The streets were filled with stalls selling dresses and suits, snacks, and toys; in between them, street vendors hawked balloons to young children. Chinese posters and newspapers covered the walls of the streets and alleys.[9]

Most streets were barely wide enough for horse-drawn carriages. The narrow alleys veered off in every direction. Three- and four-story wood-frame buildings tilted at odd, precarious angles. Food stores, small garment factories, brothels, and apartments often were mixed in the same building. The housing in Chinatown was so crowded that, in some buildings, factory workers slept in shifts between their working hours. Beds were attached to walls and stacked on top of each other.[10]

After Wen's father died, the family moved to a three-story building on Dupont Street, where they lived on the third floor and rented out the other two. It was there that they faced the second tragedy of Wen's young life.

Early one morning in the spring of 1906, Wen's mother frantically woke her children before dawn and told them to hurry outside. As Wen raced through the living room, she felt the house shake and saw the chandelier swing up to smash into the ceiling. She was frightened but didn't show it; she helped her sisters outside. Her eldest sister, who had bound feet, could barely walk.

As soon as her children had gathered in the street, Wen's mother realized that she had forgotten her money box. Wen could run quickly, and her mother sent her back into the house to look for it. The house was still shaking wildly and Wen moved fast. She raced up the two flights of stairs, grabbed the box under her mother's bed, and stopped to catch her breath only after she made it back to the street safely. But then her eldest sister asked her to go inside again.

Her sister, thirteen years older than Wen, was among the last generation of Chinese women who bound their feet and wore jeweled bangles to decorate them. In the confusion of the early morning escape, she had forgotten to place the expensive bangles around her feet. Wen raced into the house again, quickly finding the jewelry in her sister's room on the third floor. But as she turned to head downstairs, the entire first floor of the house exploded in flames. Wen clutched the jewelry and leaped over the last flight of stairs into the street. Her mother and sisters picked her up and hugged her tightly.

San Francisco (1910)

All around them, Chinatown was in flames. Wen and her family, like thousands of San Franciscans, headed for the safety of Golden Gate Park. The 1906 earthquake had destroyed most of San Francisco, leaving more than five hundred people dead or missing. Chinatown, the chaotic neighborhood where Wen Zengde had spent her first six years, was reduced to ashes and rubble.

In the park, Wen's family found her eldest sister's fiancé. He offered to take them to live with his family in Fresno, where they could stay until Chinatown was rebuilt. The next year, Wen's family returned to San Francisco.

The new Chinatown seemed even more crowded than the old. Wen's family moved into two small rooms in a boardinghouse on Sacramento Street. Many of the old businesses returned, but there were new ones, too, including an antique store four and one-half stories high that looked like a Buddhist temple. Copper bells hung from pyramids on every corner of the green tile roof and rang in the wind. There were new stores selling jade and ivory. Chinatown was again redolent with herbs, incense, and barbecued pork. But many of the opium dens had not been rebuilt and the smell of the drug had disappeared.

Wen's older brother finished college after they returned from Fresno and founded a Chinese newspaper. Wen's mother and her four sisters earned money by collecting scraps from a nearby garment factory and sewing them into pajamas. They soon moved to 914 Clay Street, near two playgrounds and the Oriental Public School. It also was close to Rev. Daniel G. C. Wu's Chinese Episcopal Church. Wen's family attended services there on Sundays, and one of her sisters would later marry Mr. Wu.

Wen became a diligent student. Her eldest sister taught her Cantonese, and she studied English with other Chinese and Japanese students at the Oriental Public School. She learned about China and the coming revolution from her brother and from teachers at an evening school run by Sun Yatsen's supporters. In 1910, she learned some lessons from Sun himself.

About a year and a half after his visit to Wen's home, Sun was again in the United States raising funds when an officers' revolt, on October 10, 1911, set off a successful revolution. Within weeks, provinces throughout China declared their independence from Manchu rule. Sun returned to China to take over, for a few months, as provisional president of the Chinese Republic.

In San Francisco, the Chinese community celebrated the victory with a parade of floats and Chinese dragons. Wen, in her finest dress, rode in the middle of a float decorated with wreaths, flags, and flowers. A sign along the side of the float proclaimed: Monarchy Is Dead! Long Live the Republic!

Wen's brother left for China to become a senator in the new government. She was eager to go to China, too. When Wen finished high school, she, her number-six sister (Wen Zuofan), and her mother boarded a Japanese liner for Shanghai. In a rare show of extravagance, Wen's mother bought first-class tickets. She wanted her daughters to feel proud when they saw China for the first time.

Wen's first look at China was from the Huangpu River as they neared Shanghai. A steam launch took them the last few miles from their ocean liner to the wharf, where she could see outlines of the banks and trading houses along the Bund, the former towpath that borders the river. Hundreds of sampans crowded the harbor, and the Bund was filled with rickshaws and coolies hauling freight from the docks. Shanghai was China's most modern city, a center of commerce that seemed as cosmopolitan as San Francisco. Flour mills, cotton factories, sawmills, and huge storage tanks owned by Standard Oil and Shell lined the riverbank.[11]

The buildings along the Bund were evidence of the power of Shanghai's foreign community. There were Renaissance-style structures like the Masonic Hall and the Banque de l'Indo-Chine, which had been completed recently. The original Jardine, Matheson warehouse, built in 1851 while the opium trade flourished, was still standing. Nearby was the German Club, which had opened in 1907, and the Russo-Chinese Bank, with elaborate statues over its entrance. In the middle of the Bund, opposite the shed where British officials collected customs duties, was the Tudor-style Custom House, built in 1893, with a high-pitched roof and a four-faced clock tower. The six-story Palace Hotel, at the corner of Nanjing Road, was among the tallest buildings on the Bund. (The region's weak subsoil limited building heights to six stories.) The Shanghai Club, which opened in 1910, had a bar, billiard room, and library where Westerners gathered.[12]

The growth of the foreign community had followed China's defeat in the Opium War. Under China's treaty with the victors, Shanghai was one of five ports opened to international trade. The Manchu rulers agreed that foreigners living in Shanghai would be exempt from Chinese laws. The foreigners established their own government and built their own wealthy and elegant community, fifteen thousand Westerners isolated from the million Chinese who lived around them. In the middle of the city, they built a recreation ground where they could bet on horse races and play golf, tennis, and cricket.

But there were still remnants of old China everywhere—hundreds of family burial mounds rose from the flat river plain, some near the tall stacks belching smoke from mills and factories. Many of the shops on busy Nanjing Road looked like the stores in Wen's Chinatown, with their hanging signs and lamps with red tassels. Some buildings featured gilded woodwork on their upper stories, portraying scenes from Chinese history.[13]

Wen would live much of her life in Shanghai, but this first visit lasted only a few days. Her brother had come to take her family north to Beijing, where Wen hoped to attend college.

TWO
Beijing
(1919)

Early one morning in May, a group of Wen's classmates cornered her in a bathroom of the women's dormitory. They lived together at the North China Union College for Women (soon to become part of Yenching University), a liberal arts school that attempted to merge Western and Chinese culture and education.[1] Wen had made many good friends among her native Chinese classmates, but today they were treating her like she was not Chinese.

"You must be sad today to be a foreigner," one of them told Wen. "The foreigners have hurt China."

Her friends lectured her about the Paris peace talks and how the foreign powers had abandoned China. They had learned that France, Great Britain, and Italy had agreed to honor their secret wartime agreements to give Japan control of Qingdao, a major port in Shandong Province where Japan had captured a German naval base. Even the Chinese government had secretly endorsed Japanese control of Qingdao. The students planned to take to the streets in protest.

Wen didn't understand why her classmates felt she shared some blame for this. She stayed in her dormitory that afternoon while more than three thousand students from thirteen Beijing colleges rallied in Tiananmen Square and then marched past the foreign embassies, carrying signs opposing the Versailles treaty.[2] The students burned the home of one cabinet minister who supported Japan and attacked the Chinese envoy to Japan. Police beat the students and attempted to break up the rally. But the students called a strike, setting off demonstrations throughout the country and a nationwide boycott of Japanese goods.[3]

The May 4 rally was the beginning of an intellectual movement to revitalize China and overcome the failure of the 1911 revolution to usher in an era of political and intellectual freedom. In the years that followed, the legacy of the May Fourth movement was adapted to serve a variety of political causes. Sun Yatsen allied himself with the students and viewed the movement as a step toward national consciousness. Chiang Kaishek twisted the May Fourth message to lend support to preserving traditional Chinese culture, the opposite of what the students had advocated. And Mao Zedong, who was an assistant librarian at Beijing University during the 1919 student uprising there, later cited May Fourth as one of the foundations of the Communist revolution in China. He exploited it for his own cause and, in 1966, cited it as the precursor of the Cultural Revolution.[4]

Wen's years at Yenching University placed her among a new elite emerging in China. For more than twelve hundred years, Chinese higher education had been designed to prepare scholars for a rigorous series of examinations that would lead them to a life of government service. But the examination system had been abolished in 1905, and China's intellectuals now were searching for new models.[5] As national hostility toward Japanese aggression grew, educators looked to the West, particularly the United States, for guidance.[6]

After 1911 China's leaders developed a national system of schooling, with institutions of higher education organized much like colleges and universities in the West. The system included national institutions, such as Beijing University, as well as provincial and private colleges.[7] Some Western-run colleges in China, founded to spread Christianity, adapted and, like Yenching, became leading institutions of secular education.[8]

College graduates became part of a small, modern elite. Initially, very few of them were women. Government primary schools first admitted women in 1911, and by 1922 there were only 405 women enrolled among the 10,000 students attending China's national universities.[9]

The educated class, particularly those who had studied abroad, had great influence over the movement to transform and develop China.[10] But their status, and their foreign ideas and manners, also alienated them from the average Chinese, a conflict that would continue throughout the twentieth century in China.

Wen graduated from Yenching after four years of studying English, history, and British and American literature. She had been proud and independent, despite her occasional differences with her classmates. After college her brother, Wen Xingfei, still a government official, introduced her to Beijing high society. She spent her days studying Chinese calligraphy and her evenings at dancing parties. Wen felt like a princess; her lively spirit attracted many admirers.

Chen Xiaowei was Wen's thirteenth suitor, and, from all appearances, he was not a lucky man. On their second date, he came to call in his finest outfit, a dark silk Chinese robe. Wen was a modern woman; she was not impressed. She wrinkled her nose in disapproval and told him he looked old-fashioned. So Chen retired to a sitting room after he sent one of his servants to buy him a Western-style suit. When he greeted Wen a second time, she seemed to be suppressing a laugh. The pants looked baggy and the sleeves were far too short. But, for once, she held her tongue.

Wen certainly was different from all the polite, shy Chinese girls Chen had courted. She was intelligent and strong-willed, not afraid of a good argument. She was not as beautiful as other women he knew, but Chen was looking for a wife he could talk with, not stare at. Besides, Chen could always find beautiful young girls who would spend an afternoon or evening with him for a small price. He was no stranger to Beijing's brothels.

There were many other men competing for the affections of this slightly built, sharp-tongued young woman who had been born in America. Chen was a man of some importance in the new government, as well as a decorated lieutenant general and a graduate of the influential Beiyang Naval Academy, but he was not handsome or rich enough to gain Wen's affections easily. He was, however, a man of remarkable charm and persistence. He was also a friend of the family. Chen and Wen's brother both were officials in the system of soldiers and politicians who were part of the constantly changing power structure of Chinese government.

The military, as much a network of families and friendships as a fighting force, was the only constant as a series of new governments collapsed. Military factions formed alliances among the warlords and held key posts in all of the governments. The warlords, who seized most revenues to support their armies, left the central government only enough money to provide jobs for their friends and relatives and to make most officials wealthy men. Corruption was endemic.[11]

Wen Xingfei, Wen's elder brother, had been elected to the legislature in 1912–13 under President Yuan Shikai. (Sun

Yatsen had resigned in favor of Yuan in 1912 but Yuan betrayed the Republic and dissolved parliament. Yuan died in 1916, shortly after his unsuccessful attempt to become emperor.) Wen Xingfei remained active in government and served as secretary to Wang Chongwei, a graduate of Beiyang and Yale University. Wang had drafted Sun's statement on the goals of the Chinese revolution and became a major player in the series of new governments after Yuan's death, first as minister of justice and eventually as premier for a brief term.[12] As Wang's power grew, Wen took on various positions in the communications and finance ministries, among others. One of his colleagues was a young Beiyang graduate named Chen Xiaowei.

Chen's mentor was another cabinet official, Jin Yunpeng. Jin had been a military adviser to Yuan Shikai but later helped defeat him. After Yuan's death, Jin was one of the most influential of the Beiyang graduates in the central government. His fortunes shifted as the regional warlords battled for power—he served as premier twice and resigned both times, finally retiring from politics at the end of 1921 to become a businessman and then a Buddhist monk.[13]

Chen remained part of the permanent class of bureaucrats, like Wen's brother, and served in office throughout the turmoil. They worked together in the Ministry of Communications, which was in charge of receipts from the railways, telegraph, postal, and shipping services. The ministry also handled loans from foreign governments and businesses.[14] Chen and Wen Xingfei often crossed paths. In both politics and courtship, friendships and family relationships were of the highest importance.

Chen's position earned him the respect and friendship of Wen's brother. His polite, soft-spoken manner won over Wen's mother, sisters, and even the family cook. Everyone in the family loved him, but it took him six months—and a twenty-karat diamond engagement ring—to convince Wen to marry him.

They were married at the Navy Club in the spring of 1922. Wen wore a long white gown, and Chen was dressed in an elegant tuxedo. He spared no expense to entertain the rich and powerful guests from Beijing society who came to celebrate the occasion.

After the wedding, they lived for a short time in an expensively furnished, modest home in the western suburbs of Beijing. In a few months, they moved to a house where they could, literally, live like royalty. The home, on Wang Fujing Dajie, was owned by a former prince who was short of money. He rented Chen half of his 120-room mansion, replete with a glassed-in bamboo forest, a small temple for the goddess of mercy, and fifty servants.

Wen hosted dinner and dancing parties for the generals and officials with whom Chen worked, hiring musicians from the Beijing Hotel to play Western music. She developed a taste for fine furniture, antiques, jewelry, and expensive clothes. And Wen learned how to gamble, playing in the high-stakes card games that were a feature of many parties.

She never had to worry about money. Chen's fortune seemed limitless. After they were married, he used his connections to open the Beijing Savings Bank, one of the new-style banks that the government authorized to issue money. Wen helped find depositors for the banks by attending parties with warlords' wives and convincing them to open new accounts.

The banks paid high interest rates to attract depositors. To pay the interest, they reinvested money in speculative instruments, such as highly volatile government bonds.[15] Chen's political contacts—he still held a variety of government posts—helped him follow the markets closely.

Chen also maintained his contacts with another side of Beijing society. Prostitution was legal in the capital—brothels even advertised in the newspapers—and, for thousands of young women, it was the only means of support in a society that still had little respect for women. Prostitution was also a major source of revenue for the gangs and secret societies that flourished under the weak governments.[16]

Wen tried to ignore Chen's indiscretions. The couple grew apart as he spent less and less time at home. Wen also was away often, spending most of her evenings at card parties. She pursued gambling as Chen pursued women. But Chen's pursuit could be more dangerous. One night, his driver tracked Wen down at a card game and brought her an urgent message. He whispered that Chen's life was being threatened and asked her to come with him.

The chauffeur drove Wen quickly through Beijing neighborhoods she had never seen and parked in an alley behind a rambling wood apartment building. On the second floor, Wen saw Chen.

He was on his knees, naked, in the middle of a dark living room that smelled of cheap perfume and incense. A soldier stood behind him, pointing a gun at his head. From what Wen could gather, they had been competing for the affections of the same prostitute, and the soldier had found Chen and the prostitute in bed together. The young woman sobbed hysterically as the soldier waved his pistol in the air and yelled curses at Chen.

Wen talked softly to the soldier and at first offered him money, which seemed to make him even more angry. Wen decided that she would have to drop names, as embarrassing as it was. She quietly informed the soldier about Chen's position and his links to leading government officials. He backed away, grabbed the prostitute by the elbow, and left.

Chen and Wen never talked about the incident. It apparently did little to change Chen's habits. Their marriage seemed only a formality. But another crisis—this time a financial one—drew them together.

Their bank always had been a risky venture, but by 1925, three years after they founded it, it was in serious trouble. The central government's ability to collect revenues had continued to shrink, and the government began to default on some of its bonds. Chen and Wen managed to keep the bank afloat as other banks failed. But when they discovered the bank manager had been embezzling funds, a collapse seemed inevitable.

Chen and Wen liquidated most of their personal assets to pay off depositors. They sold their jewelry—Wen discreetly pawned it with the help of her sister's husband—moved into a small house, and auctioned their furniture. Wen was even forced to pawn her twenty-karat engagement ring.

By 1926 the bank had failed, and Chen's government positions also seemed tenuous. Chen and Wen prepared to leave Beijing and move south to Shanghai.

A year earlier, Shanghai had been the site of another student-led rebellion against the foreign powers. On May 30, 1925, Sikhs from the foreign-run Shanghai Municipal Police broke up a student demonstration, killing thirteen persons. Three weeks later in Canton, British and French marines killed another fifty-two demonstrators. The attacks set off nationwide strikes and boycotts of foreign goods.[17]

In 1926–27, a young general named Chiang Kaishek emerged to lead an expedition from Canton to the north, defeating warlord armies and winning support from patriotic, antiforeign students, merchants, and workers along the way. Chiang, who had rescued Sun Yatsen from a Canton warlord and had become Sun's military leader, claimed Sun's legacy after his death in 1925. As his army swept north, Chiang showered the country with propaganda to promote his leadership.[18] His victories brought hope to those who once again dreamed of a unified republic.

Before reaching Shanghai, however, Chiang double-crossed the Communist-led labor unions that had taken control of the city from the foreign troops. He conspired with Shanghai gangs to kill thousands.[19]

Soon after they arrived in Shanghai, Wen gave birth to her first child, a girl. They called her Shi Qui, or Lela, and Wen spoiled her. But Chen continued to visit brothels and to have affairs with other women, while Wen remained at home. They spent little time together and seemed to fight whenever they saw each other. In fits of anger, Wen would sometimes throw priceless Ming vases at her husband, smashing them against the walls.

Not long after Lela was born, Wen's sixth sister, Wen Zuofan, who had come with her and their mother to China and married a mining engineer from Canton, gave birth to her seventh daughter. Unable to raise another child on her husband's salary, she planned to send the child to an orphanage. But Wen's mother asked her to adopt the newborn girl. Some of the servants said that Wen's family had another motive for the adoption. They hoped a second child would keep Chen and Wen from fighting so much. Wen called her adopted daughter Shi Jun, or Elsie.

Wen was often a strict mother. When her daughters were learning to walk, she made sure they stood up straight and checked the soles of their shoes to see if they were wearing evenly. Sometimes, she would secretly watch the girls climb the stairs and sneak up behind them, hitting them on the ankles with a backscratcher if they slouched. The most important thing for a young girl to learn, Wen told her daughters, was good manners. She punished them harshly when they misbehaved.

On weekends, Wen often took Elsie to see her godmother, one of the matriarchs of the Sassoon family. The Sassoons were a family of Sephardic Jews, originally from Baghdad, who had founded a trading company in Shanghai in the 1850s and now owned much of the city's real estate. Elsie's godmother, a frail, elderly woman, lived in the Sassoon mansion in Hongqiao, a western suburb of Shanghai.

During one visit when Elsie was still a young girl, Wen placed her adopted daughter in an antique chair while she talked with Mrs. Sassoon. Elsie was hungry and hot and annoyed by all the cats and dogs that surrounded her, panting and meowing and drooling. Wen, sitting on the brocade couch on the other side of the table chatting with Mrs. Sassoon, seemed too busy to pay any attention. Elsie climbed down from the chair and crawled toward the table. A sweet New Year's dumpling was nearly within reach.

It was just then that she seemed to realize her mother was watching. But Elsie didn't stop. She grabbed a dumpling, splashed it in the dish of soy sauce—which tumbled over and spilled—and retreated to her chair to stuff the dough and red-bean paste in her mouth. Wen continued her polite conversation without pausing, staring at Elsie for only a second. But Elsie was in trouble.

As their driver took them home from the Sassoon mansion later that afternoon, Wen said nothing. But when they got inside their house, Wen called the cook to the kitchen. She sent him to bring back two huge bottles of soy sauce.

Wen opened the bottles and ordered Elsie to drink them. It was a daunting task for a young girl, but Elsie feared her mother more than she hated the salty taste. She gulped down each bottle as quickly as she could, trying not to choke. Wen looked on indignantly, hoping to teach her daughter a lesson in good manners. But what Elsie really learned was to hate the taste of soy sauce. She didn't use any for years.

Wen's stern disposition with her children may have reflected her own unhappiness with Chen and her life in Shanghai. Although Shanghai was an exciting city in the late 1920s and early 1930s, Wen favored Beijing. In Shanghai, she always kept a picture on her wall of the prince's palace where they had lived in Beijing.

Chen and Wen lived in the residential district of the French Concession, one of the nicest neighborhoods in Shanghai. Wealthy Russians, British, French, Germans, Americans, and Chinese had built huge mansions with red-tile roofs there, surrounded by high walls. Like the nearby International Settlement, the French Concession had its own government and police force, controlled by foreigners. Most of the streets had French names, such as Avenue Joffre and Avenue du Roi Albert.

Much of Shanghai had changed dramatically since Wen's first arrival there. Along the Bund, many old structures had been replaced by modern hotels, banks, and office buildings. The new Custom House tower was ten stories high, and the Sassoons were building an eleven-story hotel and office tower to replace the old Palace Hotel at Nanjing Road and the Bund.[20] (New construction methods now made it possible to build Manhattan-style skyscrapers in Shanghai, despite the poor subsoil.) The city still had the best shops and restaurants in China, and much more nightlife than Beijing, but Wen preferred the quiet, civilized pace of the northern capital.

By the 1930s, Chiang Kaishek headed a Nationalist government that was layered with the same type of bureaucracy that had isolated the emperors. He used censorship and brutal suppression of the opposition to solidify power. Chiang, with the help of Nazi military advisers, moved China toward fascism.[21]

The Communist party, meanwhile, had been decimated by

Chiang's armies and moved its base to the hills. Rejecting Soviet advice to organize the urban proletariat, it found support among the peasants. Mao Zedong, a native of Hunan Province who was among the organizers of the party in 1921, became a driving force. He urged peasants to overthrow their landlords and helped form a peasant army schooled in guerrilla warfare.[22]

Foreign aggression brought the Nationalists and Communists together in an uneasy alliance. Japan had seized Manchuria in 1931 and set up a puppet government. In July 1937, following a possibly staged incident at a rail junction outside Beijing,[23] Japan launched a full-scale invasion. The Nationalists at first did battle in the cities. In Shanghai, German-trained Chinese troops fought the Japanese for three months, suffering 270,000 casualties. The Japanese took more than 40,000 casualties. Thousands of civilians were killed, and much of Shanghai outside the foreign settlements was devastated by shelling from Japanese warships. The Chinese troops retreated to Nanjing, which fell easily to the Japanese. Then, in a horrifying seven-week campaign against Nanjing's civilians, Japanese troops murdered at least 42,000 Chinese. Many of them were buried alive or doused with kerosene and set afire. More than 20,000 Chinese women were raped.[24]

By then, Chen and Wen had fled Shanghai, seeking safety in the British colony of Hong Kong.

THREE
Hong Kong
(1936)

 Tiny, prosperous Hong Kong seemed safe from Japanese attack. The British had ruled the island for nearly a century, first claiming it after their victory in the Opium War. Kowloon became part of the colony in 1860; the New Territories were added in 1898. Under Chinese control, Hong Kong had been a nearly barren island, but it flourished as a British colony and base for the East India Company's opium trade. During periods of unrest in China, new waves of immigrants settled there, mostly as a work force for British industry. By the late 1930s, a million people lived in Hong Kong and it was becoming a major industrial center.[1]

Chen and Wen would enjoy five relatively peaceful years in the colony. Chen began a career as a newspaper editor, Wen started teaching for the first time, and their only son, Kuo Chen (or Daniel), was born there.

After their first few months in Hong Kong, they rented a big house on renowned Victoria Mountain, overlooking Repulse Bay. They hired eight servants, including amahs for each of the children and two cooks. The big living room had an antique piano in the center, modern Western furniture, and Chinese art and sculpture, including several three-foot-high white porcelain horses. The house also had five bedrooms, three baths, a formal dining room, and a large, enclosed balcony that served as Chen's study.

Early each morning, Chen would sit at his desk overlooking the bay and read the calligraphy his children had prepared for him the night before. Their usual assignment was to write a passage of Buddhist teachings or scriptures in Chinese characters. Before the children ate breakfast, they reported to Chen's desk, where he handed them their work marked with red pen. He was very formal with his children, but there was warmth and gentleness behind his strict manner.

After Chen left for work, Wen would talk with the children and have them read articles from Chen's newspaper out loud. The stories of the Japanese atrocities scared them—the two girls often had nightmares about the cruel Japanese soldiers.

Chen worked in Kowloon as editor of the *Observatory Review,* a semiweekly newspaper he had founded in November 1936.[2] He wrote historical essays, poems, and editorials about international affairs. His writing was an odd mix of Buddhist pacifism and hardnosed politics. Seeing both the Japanese and the Communists as his enemies, Chen remained loyal to Chiang Kaishek and wrote editorials advising him on military tactics.

The tabloid sold well—about ten thousand copies per issue—despite the growing number of competing papers. Thousands of copies were sent to China, where it was read widely in the high schools.

Wen worked at the paper, too, reading page proofs and balancing the books, but she worked different hours from Chen and they rarely saw each other at the office. Several days a week, she taught remedial English to Filipinos, Malaysians, Thais, and other foreigners.

Elsie and Lela attended a girls' school during the day and studied piano and ballet in the afternoons. The girls also played with their animals, the birds, ducks, chickens, and other pets in the courtyard of their home. None of the animals seemed to live very long, but Wen bought new ones when a pet died or ran away. When one duck that had survived as a pet for several years broke its foot, Wen and Elsie took it to a Buddhist temple that cared for crippled animals. The monks conducted a long, elaborate ceremony to pray for the duck, and they were happy to leave the pet in their care.

On most evenings, Wen and Chen left home separately, Wen to go to gambling parties and Chen to be with his girlfriends. Wen dressed elegantly in silk, open-backed dresses pinned at the small of her back with diamonds or emeralds. In the winter, she wore white fox furs. Wen gambled excessively and sometimes drank heavily, but never seemed to get drunk or run out of money.

During the summers, when the children were not in school, Wen would take them to the Repulse Bay beach nearly every day with baskets of fruit and iceboxes filled with barbecued pork and duck. The children played on the beach while Wen sat inside a tent with her hat on, chain-smoking cigarettes, eating chocolates, and reading books and magazines. When the children stopped by her tent, Wen would talk to them about the latest Errol Flynn movie or discuss politics.

After lunch, the children often walked to the Repulse Bay Hotel, where they invariably found their father in the lobby or on the veranda. He always was dressed in formal party attire and surrounded by a bevy of young girlfriends. Chen would greet the children, the girlfriends would smile at them, and Chen would give them some money to buy ice cream and soda. Wen never went with the children to the hotel.

Wen had known for some time that Chen's infidelities hadn't ended once they left China. But instead of visiting prostitutes, Chen now spent time with four or five mistresses, all of them young enough to be his daughters. Wen convinced herself she wasn't jealous and tried to live her own life.

But when one of her friends told her that Chen had fathered a child with one of the mistresses, Wen felt she had to do something. The mistress was a teahouse waitress who lived in a poor section of the city. One day, Wen visited her unannounced and found her holding a six-month-old son who looked exactly like Chen. The girl was friendly and they talked openly.

A few days later, Wen returned to the girl's house with some money, clothes, and jewelry as gifts. Perhaps Wen felt some sympathy for this girl, a single mother at such a young age. Or perhaps she felt compelled to show that she was in charge, that Chen Xiaowei had only one real wife and her name was Wen Zengde. Over the next few weeks, she tracked down Chen's other mistresses. She began to visit each of them once a month, bringing them all money and gifts. Her husband thought her visits to his mistresses amusing; Wen's friends were baffled by her behavior. But in her own way and on her own terms, Wen remained in control.

Late in 1941, the Japanese prepared to open new fronts in the war. Chen burned all his papers and notes at the newspaper office, then fled by fishing boat, wearing a disguise. From the new Nationalist capital at Chongqing, under constant bombardment from Japanese planes, he continued to publish his newspaper.[3] After he settled there, he sent for the teahouse girl and her baby. But Chen wrote Wen that he didn't think Chongqing would be safe for her and her three children.

Wen and the rest of the family remained in Hong Kong. They were at home on December 8 when the Japanese bombed nearby Kai Tak airport, the same day (Asian time) they attacked Pearl Harbor. For the next two weeks, Wen and the children watched from their balcony as the Japanese planes attacked Kowloon. They could hear the bombs hit the city. Soon, the air raid sirens on their side of the island blared almost every day and the family and servants headed for the air raid shelters, long, low tunnels dug into the mountain. They spent most of their nights there, huddled with hundreds of others on blankets on the floor. The overhead light bulbs were too dim for reading, so they all tried to sleep through the ceaseless noise of diving planes and exploding bombs that shook the ground.

On Christmas Day, Wen and the children watched destroyers flying Japanese flags enter Repulse Bay. The ships fired their guns, but there was no response. A white sheet waved above the military base on Garden Road. The few British and Canadian troops that remained had retreated; the Japanese seized Hong Kong with no resistance.[4]

Wen knew that her daughters would not be safe from the invading Japanese troops. The girls also understood—they had read the newspapers and heard stories from the servants about Japanese soldiers raping young girls. Wen cut their hair and dressed them in boys' clothes. As the Japanese moved from house to house, Wen hid them under the beds, wrapped in straw mats, or in big jugs in the cellar.

Wen rarely left the house. There were few places to go—all the banks, markets, and stores, even the hospitals, were closed. The troops interrogated anyone on the streets and shot or bayoneted people who did not bow when they approached a Japanese soldier. One of the girls' schoolmates was shot after she left her house. Wen's daughters lived in fear, but the constant hiding was hard on them. They needed to stretch or walk around the house after a few hours under the beds or in the cellar.

One day about a week after the invasion, the girls were sitting with Wen in the living room when they heard a loud knock at the door. A soldier outside was shouting "Hua gu niang!" the phrase for young virgins. The girls trembled, but Wen headed straight for the door. She greeted four soldiers in yellow uniforms and invited them inside. They seemed very young and not as mean-looking as the troops Wen had seen on the streets.

As the girls sat in silence, too frightened to speak, Wen spoke with the soldiers. One of them asked her if there were any young girls living there. No, Wen told him, only her three sons. He looked at them carefully, but the girls' short hair and baggy clothes didn't draw his suspicion. He nodded and turned to leave, saying they would return later to search the house.

Wen was now convinced that it was time for them to escape Hong Kong. She planned to take the children to a small village in Guangxi Province, where her brother had a fish farm and her mother now lived. The area was remote enough to be safe from the Japanese. But they would have to cross a heavily guarded river that separated Hong Kong from the Chinese border in Shenzhen.

The next day, Wen moved the children to the home of her number-six sister (Wen Zuofan, Elsie's real mother) in Kowloon, not far from the river. Wen's sister was weak from her long struggle with cancer—she would die a few days after Wen and the children escaped—but she helped Wen find a fisherman to take them across. Wen offered to pay him well, half before the escape and half when they reached the other side.

Hong Kong (1936)

Two days later, around midnight, she dressed the children in peasants' clothes and blackened their faces. She warned them to be completely silent and to lie still when they crossed the river. The trip would be dangerous, she said, but if they stayed in Hong Kong they were certain to be killed by Japanese soldiers. Before they left, Wen wrapped a gold chain—one of the few valuable possessions she had left—around Elsie's waist.

The moon was covered by clouds that night, and it was almost too dark to see. Wen carried Daniel in her arms and the two girls followed, holding each other's hands. Near the river, they met the fisherman, who nodded to them but did not speak. He led them under a barbed-wire fence and down the bank to his boat. Then he signaled them to remain silent and pointed up the hill, a few hundred yards away, where a giant searchlight blinded their eyes as it scanned the banks and the river.

The boat was small and the fisherman would need to make two trips. Wen went first with Daniel, showing her daughters how to lie down across the bottom of the boat. The fisherman rowed quickly and quietly. Each time the searchlight passed, he lay down, too, as the boat coasted in the current.

After Wen and Daniel reached the opposite bank, the fisherman returned for Elsie and Lela. Wen waited in the dark for what seemed like an hour. She could hear shots being fired from the hillside, but none of them came near the boat. Elsie later told her mother she had held her breath all the way across. At the riverbank, the girls climbed out of the boat and ran to hug their mother. Wen thanked the fisherman and paid him. That night, Wen and the children found lodging in a small village near the river. They slept in a mud hut with a straw roof. Their journey to Guangxi would begin the next morning.

FOUR
Guangxi Province
(1942)

 Wen could see the men approaching as soon as she and her children stepped outside the dusty inn where they had spent the night. They appeared at first to be soldiers, in their khaki Nationalist uniforms with jodphur leggings, curved swords, and long-handled Mauser pistols hanging from their gunbelts. But they were swaggering instead of marching. Wen easily recognized them for what they were: a hardened gang of peasant bandits.

Since the Japanese invasion, bandits—many of them former soldiers—dominated much of the rough countryside, roaming at will in areas where government control was weak or nonexistent. Some had been farmers whose land was destroyed by the Japanese; others were simply deserters who left their units to escape the starvation, disease, and poverty suffered by most Nationalist troops.[1]

Many of the bandits smuggled opium, retreating across the provincial or national borders when they were pursued.[2] Some gangs made money by forcing travelers to pay protection fees to pass through their territory. Often, they kidnapped children of rich parents to collect ransom money.[3] From the way this group of ruffians was eyeing her five-year-old son, Wen sensed that Daniel was in danger.

The leader of the gang stepped forward to talk with Wen. He looked her over, trying to decide if she was a wealthy woman. Wen stared back intently at him, trying to disguise her fear. He seemed so young, barely in his twenties. His eyes were glazed and distant, the look of an opium addict. Wen could barely understand his Cantonese dialect, even though it had been the first language she spoke as a child. He told Wen that they were Nationalist soldiers fighting the Japanese who had been separated from their unit.

Wen knew he was lying, but she decided to speak plainly. She explained that she and her family had escaped the Japanese in Hong Kong, lost all their possessions, and were headed to her mother's village in Guangxi. Her husband, she said, was an important general who now was a famous newspaper editor in Chongqing. Perhaps they had heard of him, General Chen Xiaowei?

Wen realized her husband's position might make Daniel an attractive catch for bandits, but she also hoped that his status—and the fact that it would be nearly impossible to collect a ransom from more than five hundred miles away during wartime—might discourage them. Wen was at least relieved that, unlike the Japanese they had just escaped, these men seemed to have no interest in the girls.

The leader told Wen they would like to take Daniel with them. The boy could take care of their boots and uniforms, and Wen would be contributing to the fight against Japan. The bandits seemed well practiced in the art of deception.

Wen decided to play along, hoping to outwit them. She said she would be happy to give them her son, but only if they agreed to adopt him. She invited the leader to go with her to a nearby temple and pray to the gods as a way to authenticate their agreement. Wen didn't realize it immediately, but she had found a way to frighten off the gang. Peasant bandits were notoriously superstitious. One of their greatest fears was kowtowing, since it reminded them of the way bandits were executed, kneeling with their heads to the ground awaiting the sweep of the sword that would decapitate them.[4]

On the way to the temple, the leader of the gang seemed very nervous. Wen pressed on, telling him how proud she would be to have him as her brother, caring for her precious son, the only male heir of the famous General Chen. By the time they reached the temple gate, the gang leader's face was covered with sweat. Perhaps, he said, this wasn't such a good idea; the boy seemed young and somewhat frail. The bandit nodded his head quickly, thanked Wen for her offer, and led his men away. Wen's quick wit had saved her family once again.

The rest of the trip through the countryside was less eventful, a series of long, exhausting walks from town to town, through the marshes in Guangdong and into the hills of eastern Guangxi Province. On some days, they were lucky enough to get rides on the back of a passing truck. Further east, they traveled by riverboat. Their destination was a small town called Teng Xian, southwest of Wuzhou along the Xun Jiang River, where Wen's brother owned a fish farm. It took almost two months to get there.

In Wuzhou, Wen took the gold necklace that Elsie had worn around her waist since they left Hong Kong and traded it for new clothes and cloth shoes for all four of them. She also bought some gifts for her mother and for her brother's family. Wen and the children looked refreshed and happy when they stepped off the boat that took them from Wuzhou to Teng Xian.

The countryside was different from anything Wen had seen before. It was filled with rivers, lakes, and man-made ponds. Deep bamboo forests surrounded the village. The sunsets seemed almost magical—a purple haze settled over the forests after the sun passed below the horizon. The natives of the region seemed magical, too, people with strange customs who were unlike any Chinese people Wen had encountered before.

Some five hundred years before Christ, as Confucius was teaching the values that would influence Chinese thought for centuries, a tribe known as the Miao began to settle in eastern Guizhou and western Hunan provinces. Some of them eventually migrated across central Guangxi Province. Their origins remain mysterious. They may have come from northwest China, descendants of a Chinese general or a small ancient feudal state. They called themselves Hmong, but the Chinese know them as Miao, sons of the soil.[5]

They developed a culture that made them quite distinct from the Chinese, but difficult to distinguish from some of the other minority tribes among whom they lived and intermarried. The Miao who lived in Guangxi were part of the tribe known as the *bai* (white) Miao because of the white, woven hemp cloth they normally wear. Like other Chinese minorities, the Miao wear colorful embroidered hats and costumes to market and for festivals.

The Chinese viewed the Miao and other minorities as culturally inferior. Accounts from Chinese travelers show disdain for Miao marriage and funeral customs.[6] The Chinese also considered the Miao people subject to Chinese rule. The Chinese word for their country—Zhongguo, or middle country—implies that it is at the center of the earth and all people are its subjects, regardless of national borders. Any people who accept the dominant culture's values and morality can then become Chinese. Because the Miao lived inside China, they were expected to assimilate and embrace Chinese culture.[7]

Miao songs and myths suggest that they view themselves as from the same family as the Chinese, but not under their control. They look at themselves as older brothers whose younger brothers have outnumbered and overpowered them.[8]

The Miao were once strong warriors and had resisted Chinese control for centuries. After a series of battles early in the twelfth century, the Chinese forced more than 125,000 Miao to surrender, then slaughtered many of them. The imperial armies were brought in for violent battles in the eighteenth century. The Miao resistance continued into the twentieth century, and their independence grew during the chaos of the warlord era.[9]

But the Nationalist government exerted its power in southern China after 1927. As more Chinese settled in the south and southwest in the late 1930s, escaping the Japanese, many Miao became tenant farmers working for Chinese landlords. Like the American Indians, some Miao became dependent on alcohol to deal with the humiliation of their conquest.[10]

Wen's brother's house was on a small mountain surrounded by fish ponds that were tended by Miao families. Different species of fish lived in each of the man-made ponds, separated by a series of dams. Despite the separation, the species often intermingled. To harvest the fish, the workers opened the dams and drained the lakes, catching the fish in giant nets. They kept the poorer-quality fish for themselves, salting and storing them. The best fish were sold at the markets.

Wen Xingfei, Wen's brother, sometimes returned for the harvest and banquet celebration, but he was rarely at the farm during the war years. He spent most of his time with the Nationalist government in Chongqing. His wife and two sons managed the fish farm in his absence. Wen's mother lived there, too, and the Miao people treated her with great respect, bringing her food during all their festivals.

Wen and her children were fascinated by the Miao, who had retained many of their old customs. The women seemed to do most of the work—farming, cooking, and marketing. Their food often was served in giant rice-flour wrappings, as big as tabletops. On market days, the women and girls dressed in colorful costumes—embroidered hats, dresses, and handbags, with flowers and figures stitched in violet, purple, pink, green, red, orange, and gold.

The men kept three or four concubines and treated them like servants. They worked hard during the harvest, but it seemed as if the men spent most of their time smoking water pipes, drinking tea, and playing cards. At the frequent Miao religious festivals, the old men played Chinese guitars and reed pipes as they sang traditional songs and told stories. At festivals, both men and women smoked tobacco and drank strong homemade wine. The Miao retained many of their old superstitions. Their religious leader was a type of shaman, who had power over the demons that brought death and disease.

The Miao were now a peaceful people, never seeming to quarrel among themselves. Wen and her children felt far away from war and violence in their days at Teng Xian. The family sometimes traveled to other villages, carried by small junks that had to be dragged along by men from the shore when the tide was low. But they heard little news of the war.

Several months after they arrived, the principal of a county school came to visit Wen and ask her if she would like to teach in his school. Wen welcomed the challenge. It was a boarding school with forty students, mostly boys. Few of them could read or write well, and they spoke with strange accents, a mixture of Miao and southern Chinese sounds.

Wen tried to teach them English from readers the school had collected, but she also tried to expand their understanding of the outside world. She talked about history, politics, and women's struggle for equality. The students greeted her talks with curiosity and politeness. Their parents, who paid the teachers with rice, vegetables, and pig meat twice a month, treated Wen with reverence.

But the spring floods in 1943 seemed ominous. The waters overran fish ponds, taking the fish with them to the rivers, where almost all were lost. That summer, Wen's mother fell ill. She was nearly eighty, and her eyesight and hearing had been poor for years. She died quietly in her sleep.

The villagers insisted on giving her a traditional Miao funeral, a mix of Buddhist and native traditions. Wen's mother had been born a Buddhist, and Wen, who had great respect for Buddhism, felt the ceremony would be appropriate. Her mother would be sent to heaven by the people she had grown to love.

The day of her death, the shaman-priest came to the house with other priests, carrying chimes and a giant drum. They all had shaved heads and wore bright yellow robes. They played the chimes and beat the drum as they entered the house, singing Buddhist chants. Several of them sprayed water on the ground from wooden bowls and lit tall white candles. The shaman called on the dead woman's soul to arise, then killed a rooster, whose soul would lead her soul to heaven.

After Wen's mother was cremated, the family spent the next forty-nine days in the house with her ashes, surrounded by priests who beat the drum and played the chimes. During that period, according to Chinese and Buddhist tradition, her soul would be assigned a new life. Each time a visitor came, the family members knelt by her ashes and cried. The children could barely wait for the burial.

On the forty-ninth day, the shaman led a procession to the gravesite. They carried her picture and her ashes and a large cloth with Buddhist sayings, followed by men playing instruments, dancing, and carrying bamboo twigs, all symbolic of their ancestral roots in the forest. Each of the mourners left some food and drink near the grave to satisfy the hungry ghosts whose souls had gone to hell.[11]

The funeral marked the end of the peaceful days in Teng Xian. One of Wen's nephews brought word that Japanese troops were nearing the village. The Japanese reportedly were preparing for a new offensive in south-central China. Wen's nephew took Elsie with him to Kunming to live with her father. Wen and her two remaining children planned to escape deeper into the hinterland.

For the next nine months, the Japanese would sweep through the countryside. In Guangxi Province, where Wen and her family lived, more than 100,000 people were killed, 160,000 wounded, and 300,000 homes destroyed during the war. Most of the casualties occurred during the 1944 attacks, known as the Ichigo offensive.[12]

As the Japanese attacked, Wen and her children moved with the county school into the hills and mountains of Guangxi. They made temporary quarters each time they settled, ready to move again when the Japanese army neared.

Wen's lessons reflected the times. She taught the children about slavery in America and told them the Japanese planned to make the Chinese their slaves. Her daughter Lela painted pictures every week about the war, some portraying the horror of the Nanjing massacre. All this seemed distant to the other schoolchildren. They adapted easily to their new environment. Wherever they moved, local farmers found meat and vegetables to bring to the school.

Guangxi Province (1942)

Despite the constant threat from the Japanese, Wen and her children felt at peace in the mountains and dark forests where they now lived. They were almost disappointed when word arrived that the Japanese had surrendered in August 1945. Wen and several other teachers returned to Teng Xian, leaving the children behind until they were sure the village was safe.

The village was eerily quiet and empty. The school apparently had been used as a Japanese headquarters, possibly for the police. The Japanese had left some of their belongings, as well as their Doberman pinschers. The school workers killed and ate the dogs soon after they arrived, then went to work cleaning the building for the students' return.

Two days after Wen and the others had arrived in Teng Xian, one of the workers reported a gruesome discovery to the school principal. Word spread among the teachers, villagers, and workers, and they all gathered behind the main classroom building to stare into a pit the worker had begun to uncover.

It was about ten feet long and eight feet deep. The bodies of dead civilians—men, women, and a few children—had been tossed there. Some were missing heads, arms, and legs. Others appeared to have been strangled, their eyes bulging and their tongues hanging out. Lime powder had been poured over the bodies in 'a hasty attempt to destroy the evidence. Several of the teachers screamed at the sight; one fainted, nearly falling into the pit. Wen shuddered.

The workers began removing the bodies for burial. As they dug deeper, they found new layers of corpses, covered by planks and dirt. By the time they finished, the workers had dug up more than one thousand bodies. The Japanese had massacred nearly the whole population of the village and surrounding farms.

FIVE
Hong Kong
(1955)

 In the spring of 1955, Wen received a letter at the office of her husband's newspaper from Zhou Enlai, the premier of China. Zhou had written to ask her, an American-born English teacher, aged fifty-five, to return to China to teach. In his speeches, the premier had been calling on exiled intellectuals to return. (Early in 1956, Zhou delivered a major address arguing that intellectuals were indispensable to the success of China's modernization and urging the Communist party to welcome returning exiles and treat them well.)[1] He also had written hundreds of letters to people like Wen. She discovered that Zhou was as charming in his letter as he was said to be in his public appearances. China needs people like you, Zhou wrote Wen, if it hopes to modernize, overcome years of poverty, and unify the country. Wen was flattered.

Chen, despite his bitter opposition to Wen's interest in returning to China, had helped arrange the invitation. When he realized his wife was determined to return, he knew from all their years together—and apart—that he could not change her mind. So he did what he could to guarantee her safety. Chen wrote to an old friend from his Republican government days, Zhang Xiruo, who was Minister of Higher Education and close to Zhou. Zhang was only too happy to help Wen. In addition to his friendship with Chen, he also was indebted to Wen. Zhang had visited Hong Kong frequently in the 1950s, reportedly to win support from people like Chen for the war in Korea.[2] But it was widely known that he also came to visit his concubine. When Zhang's wife found out about his infidelity, Zhang asked Wen for help in talking with her. A few years later, Zhang returned the favor when he recommended Wen to Zhou.

But even after the letter arrived, Chen tried to convince Wen not to go.

"Everyone there is a spy," Chen said the afternoon the letter arrived, "and they know I am an anti-Communist. They will treat you as a Nationalist spy because of me."

"Then why don't you come, too, and show your support?" Wen asked. It wasn't the first time he'd been asked—Zhang also had urged Chen to return and see how much good the Communists were doing for China.

"As soon as I cross the border in Shenzhen," Chen told Wen, "my mouth would be on the back of my head." It was a Chinese idiom—it meant he would be executed.

After the defeat of the Japanese in 1945, Chen and Wen had been reunited in Shanghai. Their marriage remained a formality, and Chen frequently traveled to Hong Kong to be with his teahouse girl. He moved back there permanently a few years later, anticipating the Communist victory in the civil war. Chen feared retribution for the strong pro-Nationalist and anti-Communist essays he had published in the *Observatory Review*.

Before he left, Chen gave his family the names of two

people who could help them should they be captured by the Communists. One was an assistant chief of staff in the Nationalist army; the other was the top Nationalist representative to the American embassy.

"Tell your captors these two men are your good friends," Chen told them.

"But they are both Nationalists," Wen said. "How would that help us?"

Chen laughed. "They are both Communist double agents," he said.

Wen and Daniel left for Hong Kong shortly after Chen. But Lela remained in China to continue her studies at Lingnan University in Canton. Her pro-Communist teachers, some of them Americans, had helped convince her that Communism would be good for China, and she saw no reason to leave.

The Communists had taken over the government in 1949 with wide popular support, ending years of war and economic chaos. In their first months in power, the economy improved rapidly, public transportation was restored, the spread of disease was slowed, women were given equal rights, and crime, prostitution, and corruption were virtually eliminated. In the countryside, the land reform movement ousted and executed landlords and returned power to the peasants. The public rallied behind the idealism of their new leaders.[3]

In Hong Kong, Chen rented a house on Brown Street near Causeway Bay. He lived on one side of the house with his mistress, their children, and his mistress's sister; Wen and Daniel moved into a third-floor apartment on the other side of the house.

Wen taught English at Hong Kong University and helped Chen run the *Observatory Review*. He continued to publish editorials criticizing the Communists and frequently sent letters to world leaders with copies of his articles.

Daniel attended the Peichow School in Hong Kong. Wen thought he would get a good education there, but she also knew the faculty was dominated by pro-Communists. It wasn't long before Daniel and his father began arguing over Communism. Daniel was impressed by the early successes of the new regime in China and drawn to the Communists' idealistic proclamations supporting human rights and opposing U.S. imperialism. Chen told him the Communists would bring much suffering to China and their planned economy would not work. He predicted the Nationalists on Taiwan would be more democratic and prosperous than the Communists on the mainland.

But Chen didn't try to impose his will on Daniel and encouraged him to pursue his own goals. "Perhaps you will discover twenty or thirty years from now that I was ahead of my time," Chen said. "Communism is not good for the Chinese people, but you need to find out for yourself." Two years after they had returned to Hong Kong, Daniel left for China to attend a military academy of the People's Liberation Army and train to become a communications officer.

After Daniel left, Wen began to think that she, too, might return to China. She wanted to be with her children, despite what Chen had told her. Wen saw no reason to fear the Communists; she remained strangely naïve. After she saw a magazine picture of the notorious Number One Detention House in Shanghai without guards at the front gate, she told a friend that Communist China must be a special place if the prisons had no guards. She told another friend that she thought the Communists were a lot like the Catholics—they both had confession.

But Elsie, Wen's adopted daughter, who was studying in Japan, wrote her that going to China would be "a river of no return." She would have to end all contact with her family outside China, Elsie warned, to protect herself as well as her relatives. The division between pro- and anti-Communists among overseas Chinese was so great, Elsie wrote, that she would no longer be able to stay in touch with Wen if she returned. Simply writing to Wen would put her on the side of the Communists, and she would be shunned by her friends and her own family. When Wen wrote that she would be going to China in a few months, Elsie telephoned to try to discourage her one last time.

Wen did have worries about returning to China. But she had even stronger motives for leaving Hong Kong. Now that Daniel was gone, Wen hated living alone in her apartment in the same house Chen shared with his mistress and their family. She felt angry every time the mistress brought her tea and bowed to her. Wen still thought of Chen's mistress as a concubine and a teahouse girl, even though she called herself Mrs. Chen. And Chen was never going to change his ways. He now had two more mistresses in town, sisters who lived separately and were both college graduates, one a swimmer and the other a dancing hostess. Despite all the bad things Chen and others had told her about Communist China, Wen thought, nothing could be worse than her life in Hong Kong. The letter from Zhou added to her confidence that she was making the correct decision. When her teaching duties ended at Hong Kong University that winter, she applied for a one-way entry permit to China.

One of the most difficult problems the Communists faced in their early years in power was how to organize the nation's educational system. Many Communist leaders had criticized the system developed after 1905—when the imperial examination system was abolished—for its reliance on foreign countries and ideas. In the rural areas where the Communists developed their power base before 1949, these leaders had cultivated decentralized, practical schools that served the masses and trained party officials. At the same time, however, other leaders formed a separate, modern system of select schools training the best students. The two systems reflected the continuing conflict in Chinese education.[4]

After 1949, despite their criticism of foreign models, the Chinese Communists reorganized the nation's schools on the Soviet model, particularly in higher education. American-style liberal arts colleges, like those developed after 1911, were to be eliminated, and more students would receive technical training. Instead of preparing intellectuals for government service, the educational system would train specialists to become engineers, agricultural technicians, scientists, and doctors.[5] Following the Soviet model, the Chinese developed uniform national teaching plans, materials, and textbooks for every field, to be followed scrupulously in every classroom. A standardized national college entrance exam came into use in 1952.[6]

The new system only exacerbated the conflicts in education. The rush to educate specialists left few opportunities for workers and farmers; the imitation of the Soviet system meant renewed reliance on foreign ideas; and the focus on uniformity and technical training alienated many educators and intellectuals.

Wen was assigned to teach in the English department at the First Teachers' College in northern Shanghai. The college treated Wen with kindness and respect. When she arrived, they greeted her with a ten-course banquet attended by all the top school officials. At the banquet, Wen met Zhang Shen. Zhang had worked for the YWCA in China, and they had sent her to the United States to study for several years before 1949. Wen soon realized Zhang had been told to spy on her—Zhang sometimes would come by her apartment late at night to see what Wen was doing. But Wen didn't mind her friend's intrusions because she and Zhang both spoke English well and shared an interest in America.

Wen was the only native speaker in the department. Her American accent seemed strange to her students and fellow teachers, who were required to use Soviet texts that instructed them to speak with British accents. She was assigned to teach English conversation to second-year students, but soon came to the conclusion that the school's textbooks were inadequate. The only conversation materials in the library were based on Soviet English texts—the Russian annotations had been translated into Chinese. Wen thought the dialogues about Soviet heroes were stilted and nothing like the idiomatic American English she spoke. She spent much of her spare time writing her own dialogues.

Wen could be near her children in Shanghai. Lela had graduated from Lingnan and was teaching at the Number One Medical School. They shared an apartment near the college. Daniel had left the army and was attending the Second Teachers' College, in southern Shanghai but close enough so he could visit often.

These were prosperous days in Shanghai and teachers led privileged lives. Wen could get milk, eggs, and other foods without ration coupons. Their apartment was comfortable, and they could afford to hire a maid to do the cooking and some cleaning. Wen never liked to cook.

At the Second Teachers' College, Daniel proved to be a brilliant student, and he impressed his teachers with his original work on differential equations. He also impressed the party leaders at the school because he had worked as a communications officer for Chen Yi, a top army commander then serving as vice-premier. Daniel became a student leader. Among other things, he was responsible for supervising the student newspaper.

In 1956, the year Wen returned to China, the student

paper joined in a national campaign. Mao called it the Hundred Flowers movement, quoting the classic proverb "Let a hundred flowers bloom together, let the hundred schools of thought contend." He encouraged liberal ideas and invited intellectuals to openly criticize party policies.[7]

During the early phases of the movement, intellectuals responded cautiously. Some academics disparaged the educational system for overemphasizing technical training, Soviet methods, and political dogma. But the following year, when the party called for criticism of its own officials (or cadres), intellectuals enthusiastically exposed corrupt and incompetent bureaucrats and attacked the party.[8] Wall posters and student newspapers at universities throughout the country criticized the cadres for being arrogant, stupid, and gluttonous and disputed the need for mass rallies and political-study sessions.[9] The students also questioned college admissions policies that gave preference to qualified workers and peasants.[10]

For the first time, intellectuals publicly questioned China's strongest ally, the Soviet Union, anticipating the Sino-Soviet split that officially began in 1960. Copies of Khrushchev's "secret speech" attacking Stalin were circulated. Some intellectuals saw the USSR's 1956 invasion of Hungary as a sign of the dangers of Communism and a warning that China should move away from the Soviet model, as Yugoslavia and Poland had done, or even abandon Communism altogether. In posters and on soapboxes, student leaders argued for more democracy and even for free elections.[11]

The intellectuals had gone too far. Mao now doubted their loyalty and prepared to punish them with a vengeance.[12] The repression began in June 1957. An editorial in the *People's Daily* of Beijing suggested that right-wing intellectuals were using the Hundred Flowers movement to try to overthrow the party and return capitalism to China. "These are the people," the editorial said, "whom today we call rightists."[13] It marked the beginning of a new movement, the Anti-Rightist campaign.

In the months that followed, more than half a million students, teachers, artists, and writers were labeled rightists, which effectively destroyed their careers.[14] Many were fired from their jobs; thousands were sent to labor camps in the northeast. Their families, too, were persecuted and ostracized. The party directives gave each educational institution a quota of rightists, usually about 5 percent of their total staff. Students and teachers worked zealously to fill or exceed their quota, ferreting out so-called rightists at struggle-and-criticism sessions. Even those who had not spoken out during the Hundred Flowers movement became victims.[15]

The Anti-Rightist campaign marked an important development in Chinese politics. It greatly increased the significance of class and political labels—such as "rightist" and "bad element"—and gave local party officials more power, particularly in educational institutions. It also helped establish the roots of violence that would reach full force a decade later during the Cultural Revolution.[16]

Daniel Chen was among the victims of the Anti-Rightist campaign. Although he had not criticized the party publicly, his role as student leader put him in charge of a student newspaper that had advocated more democracy. In struggle sessions, he also was attacked for his mother's American citizenship and his father's anti-Communism. Daniel was labeled a rightist and sent to a remote labor camp in Anhui Province that manufactured machine tools.

Wen was permitted to visit her son before he left. She brought him food and vitamins. She also brought assurances that Daniel's imprisonment would be short-lived. The day before the visit, a party official took Wen to dinner and told her Daniel's case was a small matter and that he would be released in two or three years. (In 1961, he was allowed to return to Shanghai and continue his research. But Daniel would never overcome his label as a rightist; he would be forced to return to labor camp once the Cultural Revolution began.)

The Anti-Rightist campaign again exposed the deep conflicts in Chinese education and raised questions about its goals. Should China focus its limited resources on educating its brightest students, or should it provide good education for children of workers and farmers, as well as for intellectuals and party officials? Should colleges and universities train technicians and specialists, or should they offer a liberal environment for intellectual development? And should all foreign ideas and educational models be abandoned and replaced with a system designed for the unique nature of Chinese culture and society?

In the late 1950s, Mao rejected the Soviet model that had dominated education. Still angry about what he saw as disloyalty during the Hundred Flowers movement, he tried to break the intellectuals' monopoly over education. As part of the Great Leap Forward of 1958–59, he established work-study and factory-run schools. Class background became an even more important consideration for college admissions, and increasing numbers of workers' and farmers' children attended colleges and universities.

But by the early 1960s, Mao's designated successor, Liu Shaoqi, and other leaders sought to exonerate intellectuals who had been labeled rightists and again put them in control of the schools. Liu closed many of the work-study schools and provided support for schools that trained intellectuals. To placate Mao, Liu advocated a two-track system, with one group of schools for the wealthy and talented and another for the working class. But at its apex, at so-called keypoint schools, the system favored children of intellectuals and cadres.[17]

In the summer of 1958, Wen's department merged with the Shanghai Foreign Languages Institute. The institute was located in the northeast section of the city, north of Hongkou Park. The site of the campus once had been a Sikh burial ground, and the Japanese had built a school there before the war. After 1949, it became the Russian Language Training School, a name it retained until the late 1950s.

Wen lived with her daughter in a second-floor apartment provided by the school. The apartment was part of a drab, squat complex known as Friendship Village, about a fifteen-minute walk from campus. It had been constructed for the Soviets who came to teach at the school and was luxurious by Chinese standards. The three-story apartments had front- and backyards, large living rooms, two bedrooms, a porch, and two balconies. But the Soviet experts never lived there—they still preferred Shanghai's hotels. So the institute allotted the housing to its faculty and administrators. The apartments were considered to be too large for the Chinese, however, and were divided up for two or three families. Wen and Lela were given the entire second floor and shared their kitchen and bathroom with another family.

The Institute had more than two thousand students and three hundred teachers, although many of the teachers were older and semiretired. As many as forty foreigners taught there. During the Great Leap Forward, the school admitted a larger number of students from workers' and farmers' families. By the early 1960s, however, the institute had become one of China's prestigious keypoint schools, and many working-class students were weeded out by the rigorous curriculum.

The Foreign Languages Institute school was headed by a

president and vice president, who supervised the deans of the five departments: English, German-French, Arabic-Japanese, Spanish, and Russian. A middle school was also attached to the institute.[18] The real power at the school was in the hands of Communist party members, who controlled teaching assignments, housing, and the distribution of coupons for food, bicycles, and nearly every other necessity.

Wen felt less welcome at the institute than she had at the teachers' college. She was one of the few native speakers in her department. Wen taught what the Soviets called "extensive reading" to second-year students, using simplified versions of novels like *Uncle Tom's Cabin,* with the Russian notes translated into Chinese.

Wen was a demanding teacher who expected her students to be well prepared. Many students at first found her American accent difficult to understand, but most of them came to like and respect her. Yet some of the cadres in the department saw Wen's foreign background as a source of suspicion rather than an asset. Party officials occasionally chastised her for speaking with some of the foreign teachers. A few of her colleagues resented her suggestions about how to speak English correctly and insisted that Wen, not they, should speak differently. They accused her of arrogance when she resisted. Their resentment would explode into vengeful anger when the Cultural Revolution began.

Wen married Chen Xiaowei at the Navy Club in Beijing in the spring of 1922. Chen was a graduate of the Beiyang Naval Academy and a government official. A number of prominent officials attended the wedding.

By 1925, Wen Zengde and her husband were in serious financial difficulty as their bank was about to fail. They would move to Shanghai the next year. Standing at left, Wen is shown here with three of her older sisters and her mother, Wong Hou (seated). Standing beside Wen are (from left) her Number-Two, -Three, and -Five sisters.

The Wen family gathered in Shanghai in 1933 to celebrate her mother's eightieth birthday. The boys in front are the sons of the second wife of Wen Xingfei, Wen's older brother. Wen's two daughters, Lela and Elsie, are shown beside Wen's mother (seated). The others shown are (from left): Wen Xingfei's eldest son; Wen Zengde's husband, Chen Xiaowei; Wen Xingfei's second eldest son; Wen; Wen's Number-Five sister; Wen Xingfei's second wife; Wen Xingfei; Wen's Number-Two sister; her Number-Six sister, Wen Zuofan; Wen Zuofan's daughter; Wen Zuofan's husband, Walter Wong; and Wen Xingfei's grandson.

Wen taught English at Hong Kong University in the early 1950s until she was invited to return to China to teach. She is shown on the campus of Hong Kong University in 1955, the year before she returned to Shanghai.

SIX
Shanghai (August 1966)

The heat had been relentless that summer. For the past two weeks, the thermometer at the guardhouse inside the front gate had seemed stuck in the upper thirties (roughly a hundred degrees Fahrenheit). Black smoke poured from the tall stack of a nearby paint factory, adding a stinging, acidic smell to the moist, hot air. On the soccer field in the middle of the Shanghai Foreign Languages Institute campus, inside the gravel running track, a dozen students dressed in military uniforms with red armbands were shoving wooden classroom desks together to assemble a crude platform.

Wen Zengde glanced at the students from the third floor of the English department classroom building, across a tree-lined road from the field. They were attaching two long bamboo poles topped with red streamers to both ends of their makeshift platform. Three large white pieces of paper hung over the front of the platform, each painted with one Chinese character. Wen squinted to read the words: *Da Gui Hui*—"Monster-beating Assembly."

On her way to lunch, Wen walked past a glass-covered bulletin board on the sidewalk near the roadway. The students, who called themselves the Revolutionary Rebels, had put up a poster. The large, bold Chinese characters announced there would be a school meeting on the soccer field the next day to criticize the older teachers in the Spanish department. Five pieces of rope, each tied into a noose, hung from the top of the poster. "If you have monsters in your own department," the poster proclaimed, "bring them with ropes to the meeting to learn a lesson."

Wen was afraid. In the dining hall, she talked to her friend Fang Zhong, the chairman of the English department.

"What should we bring with us to the rally?" she asked. "What will happen there?"

"Bring nothing," Fang said. "Do what they ask of you."

The Revolutionary Rebels, all students from the Spanish department, had been the most radical of the student factions on campus. But like the other groups formed after Chairman Mao had unleashed the forces of the Great Proletarian Cultural Revolution, they had seemed to spend most of their time arguing among themselves and fighting with other student groups over who was a true revolutionary. As they prepared for the campuswide meeting, however, they appeared organized and determined.

The Cultural Revolution officially began in the summer of 1966. It resulted primarily from the ideas and decisions of one man, Mao Zedong. Mao was driven by a quest for revolutionary purity; his almost mythic position in Chinese society provided him with the power to launch the movement and mobilize the masses.[1]

Mao's proclamations were often deliberately ambiguous, and it still remains difficult to understand his goals for the movement. Some of the motivation was based on his distrust of both the Soviet Union and the United States. Antagonism toward the United States was fueled by the conflict with American troops in Korea and American support for Taiwan's claim to mainland China; it reached its peak with U.S. escalation in Vietnam. When the United States and the Soviet Union moved toward better relations in the late 1950s, the Sino-Soviet relationship began to deteriorate; the Soviets ended economic assistance to China in 1960. One cause of the Cultural Revolution was Mao's fear that the Chinese would become revisionists like the Soviets.[2]

Mao also hoped to use the revolution to reassert his power and destroy his critics.[3] He had aspirations for China, as well. Mao believed the country was on the verge of restoring capitalism. Reforms in the early 1960s had brought a return to private farms, material incentives in factories, a focus on urban rather than rural health programs, and the reemergence of traditional Chinese art and literature. The government bureaucracy had become overstaffed, and many local party organizations were corrupt and inefficient. In education, there was a widening gap between students from rural and working-class backgrounds and those from middle-class and cadre families. Mao yearned for a revolutionary, egalitarian society that would embrace socialism.[4]

Yet the Cultural Revolution was driven by far more than Mao's thoughts and proclamations. It exposed deep cleavages in Chinese society, set off power struggles at virtually every level, and unleashed violent forces that led to widespread anarchy and destruction—the beating, torture, and imprisonment of millions, and as many as one-half million deaths. Perhaps the most severe struggles took place at China's schools and colleges, where questions about the goals of education had yet to be resolved.

When Mao called on students to join his rebellion in 1966, he energized both their idealism and their anger at what nearly all of them saw as an unequal and unfair system. They welcomed their newfound power and importance and the opportunity to correct injustices.[5]

The Cultural Revolution began as a power struggle in Beijing and a debate over cultural reform. In May 1966, government officials began dispatching representatives to college campuses to create support for it. Nie Yuanzi, a teaching assistant in the philosophy department at Beijing University, responded by writing a wall poster that questioned the university administration's response to the Cultural Revolution. University leaders tried to suppress the dissent. But Mao intervened. He ordered that Nie's poster should be read over national radio and published in the newspapers. The university administration was subsequently reorganized.[6]

Mao's action legitimized spontaneous mass protests and campaigns against officials who opposed him. Wall posters written by students and faculty began to appear at schools and colleges throughout the country. The initial criticisms dealt with such issues as admissions criteria, curriculum, and examinations, but they soon included attacks on school leaders who were seen as opposing Mao's policies. Within weeks, school officials lost control and chaos reigned on campuses.[7]

Classes were called off in June and university enrollment was suspended. Liu Shaoqi then ordered work teams to visit high schools and colleges throughout China. The teams were told that there were large numbers of bureaucrats and faculty on each campus who should be criticized and possibly dismissed. But the party's attempt to regain control of the student movement backfired. Secret student groups, who called themselves Red Guards, organized to oppose the work teams. Most were from worker or cadre backgrounds. Competing student groups, many of whom called themselves Revolutionary Rebels, formed to oppose the Red Guards.[8]

In mid-July, as the poster campaigns and struggles between student groups continued on school campuses, Mao returned to Beijing to reassert his own vision of the Cultural Revolution. To prove his vigor, Mao (then seventy-three) stopped in Wuhan to swim in the powerful Yangtze River. Newspapers reported, in large red type, that he had swum nine miles down the river in an impossible sixty-five minutes, stopping at one point to teach a young woman the backstroke. The story, exaggerated if not apocryphal, captivated the nation. Workers, peasants, and students celebrated Mao's return with parades and firecrackers.[9]

In Beijing, he criticized the performance of the campus work teams, which were soon replaced by small groups elected by students, staff, and teachers.[10] In early August in Shanghai, at a meeting of party leaders packed with his supporters, Mao demoted and denounced those, like Liu Shaoqi and Deng Xiaoping, who had opposed him or misunderstood his goals, naming military leader Lin Biao his new successor. He then proclaimed the goal of the revolution. It was nothing less than to change the mental outlook of the whole society, to arouse the masses to liberate and educate themselves. He urged them to strike at revisionists, "reactionary bourgeois scholar despots," and those in the party who were "taking the capitalist road." About 5 percent of the people, Mao said, should be exposed as class enemies and repudiated. And he praised the radical students as "courageous and daring pathbreakers," endorsing them as the leaders of the new revolution.[11] Specific targets and tactics remained ambiguous, but within days the students were responding to Mao's call.

* * *

Wen knew from the beginning that this campaign would be different. Party officials had been among the first targets at the Shanghai Foreign Languages Institute in early June. Wall posters had reprimanded the vice secretary of the Youth League, Tang Dequan, whose father had been a landlord in Anhui Province.

In Wen's English department, the radicals initially directed their attention to Fang Zhong, the department chairman. Party officials secretly assigned three young English teachers to prepare wall posters. For two weeks in June, Wang Changrong, Hou Weirui, and Lu Guangdan disappeared from their study groups to research Fang's background. All three were ambitious, loyal party members from working-class families who saw themselves as the future leaders of the school. They knew their attacks on Fang would win them rewards.

A handful of party officials at the institute, as at most workplaces in China, controlled virtually every aspect of life, from job assignments to food and housing. Rewards were rationed on the basis of class and other political labels.[12] With such subjective standards, opportunists and sycophants like Wang, Hou, and Lu found ways to advance themselves in times of turmoil, usually by criticizing their colleagues.[13]

Wen had known Fang for nearly ten years and admired him as one of China's foremost scholars of English literature. He had once taught at Oxford and had been authorized by the government publishing house to prepare an official translation of Shakespeare's works. But he was an easy target for the young teachers. His wife had been ousted from the institute in the Anti-Rightist campaign, and he had since become a mere figurehead at the school, rarely appearing in his office.

Wang, Hou, and Lu emerged from their seclusion with dozens of posters naming Fang as a counterrevolutionary.

Those they pasted to the department walls quoted excerpts from Fang's famous translation of Chaucer's *Canterbury Tales,* somehow uncovering evidence of Fang's guilt in the six-century-old words of an English poet.

Soon there were other targets, inspired by class conflicts or simply a desire to settle old scores. There were posters criticizing Shi Songchuan, a young English teacher whose father had worked for a foreign firm, because he lacked "working-class feelings." This was another way of saying Shi had been too strict with the working-class students in his remedial English course.

There also were posters attacking Wen, who had angered Wang and other young teachers when she was assigned to evaluate their English conversation classes. Wang had used a traditional Chinese greeting, "You look fat," in one of the English conversation dialogues he had written, and Wen had embarrassed him when she told him that foreigners would consider the phrase an insult. The wall posters used loftier language, labeling Wen a "bourgeois academic authority" and belittling her for being born in the United States.

The walls of the English department soon were covered with posters listing accusations against teachers. They were so numerous that, to save paper, students and teachers wrote their slogans over used newspapers. Each classroom contained buckets of cheap, foul-smelling black ink, along with pails of thick chemical paste to attach the posters to the walls.

As the poster campaign continued, Wen and the other teachers spent their days in political study. The English teachers met in a third-floor classroom six days a week to memorize, recite, and discuss Chairman Mao's works and editorials in the *People's Daily.* Nearly all other reading material was banned. The older teachers like Wen also wrote self-criticisms, responding to the students' charges against them. Other English teachers wrote their own criticisms of

Fang, Wen, and the others, echoing the words of the three young radicals.

But the harshest campaign was directed at Song Yongqing. Song was the most brilliant of the young teachers in the department and made many of his colleagues jealous. He also had enemies among party officials, whom he often snubbed when they tried to meddle with his teaching.

A few weeks before the Cultural Revolution began, Song had lost his teaching position. He was demoted because he had broken up with his fiancée and had begun dating a student, something his fellow teachers saw as a breach of China's strict public morality. The department ordered the once-proud Song to clean the toilets near the offices of his former colleagues.

In June, when the Cultural Revolution reached the institute, Song also became a political target. Students wrote posters calling him an adulterer. As he worked, he was forced to wear a sign on his back that labeled him a "bad element." In another era, the sentence for his moral lapse might have been similar, but the building fury of the revolution made the attacks even more cruel and humiliating.

Late in June, Song left for the weekend and was missing when school started on Monday. He had gone to Qingdao, a seaside resort to the north where his parents lived. But he didn't visit them. Instead, he checked into a hotel and, for several days, drew the suspicious attention of the staff by reading English-language newspapers (which had been banned) and spending hours by himself on the beach, staring sadly at the waves. The staff reported Song to the police. By the time they arrived, Song had swallowed poison and walked into the ocean to drown himself. He wanted to be certain that his suicide succeeded. The police found his body on the beach.

Before he killed himself, Song had mailed farewell letters

to his friends. "I have no one but myself to blame for getting into this mess," he wrote to one of them. "I can't endure such humiliation. I appreciate the friendship and sympathy you have shown me."

Suicide has deep roots in Chinese history and mythology as an honorable way to die. The Chinese traditionally accepted—and even celebrated—suicides committed out of loyalty or to save face. Some believed their spirits would harass those who drove them to suicide. In ancient China, defeated military commanders earned reverence for killing themselves rather than surrendering. After the poet Qu Yuan drowned himself in a river to mourn the Qing conquest in 278 B.C., the people honored him by throwing glutinous rice dumplings into the water to distract the fish from eating his body. Many women in Chinese mythology committed suicide when they were forced to remarry or when they grieved over a loved one's death.

But the Communists saw suicide as escapism and as a disloyal act. They claimed that nearly anyone could be rehabilitated through labor and study. During the Cultural Revolution, a suicide—or even a murder labeled suicide—left a mark of shame and was viewed as proof of guilt. Friends and family members of those who killed themselves suffered from guilt by association.[14]

Song's death was the first, but by the time the Cultural Revolution ended eleven more of Wen's colleagues at the school would die from apparent suicides.

It was still moist and hot the morning of August 11 as Wen made the short walk to school from her apartment in Friendship Village. On the way, she greeted some of her neighbors who had moved their beds and kitchen tables onto the sidewalk to escape the heat inside their small apartments.

By the time Wen reported to the English department, a

crowd already was gathering on the sports field for the assembly organized by the Revolutionary Rebels. At 9 A.M., the Rebels, who had taken over the campus broadcast station earlier in the summer, announced the beginning of the meeting. The broadcast blasted from two huge loudspeakers on the makeshift platform and echoed over speakers in the dormitories and libraries and on each floor of the two long, four-story classroom buildings: "Revolutionary students, teachers, and workers! All revolutionary comrades must attend the meeting on the sports field this morning!"

Wen walked across the road and joined the older English teachers who stood near the platform. A few feet away, one of the Rebels was playing a recording of "The East Is Red," an ode to Chairman Mao ("The East is red / The sun rises / China has brought forth a Mao Zedong"), and students and teachers joined in the song. Other Rebels stood behind the lectern on the platform and shouted slogans into the microphone as they shook clenched fists in the air. The teachers and students on the field, all clutching their little red books, joined the Rebels in reading some of Mao's quotations in unison. One came from his 1927 report on peasant uprisings in Hunan Province, which had been cited at the party meeting days earlier.

"A revolution is not a dinner party," they chanted, "or writing an essay, or painting a picture, or doing embroidery; it cannot be so refined, so leisurely and gentle, so temperate, kind, courteous, restrained, and magnanimous. A revolution is an insurrection, an act of violence by which one class overthrows another."[15]

The chanting, shouting, and singing continued for an hour. Then, from behind the platform, Wen saw the tops of six cone-shaped hats moving from the Spanish department building toward the field. The chanting stopped as the crowd strained to see who was being led to the stage. Wen recognized Pu Yongnan, the chairman of the department, and five other Spanish teachers.

The three-foot-high hats, made of heavy sketch paper rolled into cones and pasted together, were marked with the words *Niu gui she shen,* representing two manlike beasts from hell in Chinese mythology, one with the head of a cow, the other with the head of a snake. The teachers' hands were tied behind their backs with rope and they wore name signs around their necks. Their names were crossed out with a red X, the way criminals' names are marked on posters in public places before they are executed. This scenario mimicked Mao's 1927 report from Hunan, in which he had described peasants overthrowing their landlords and parading them through the streets wearing tall hats.

A group of students pushed Pu and his colleagues toward the platform. An old, white-haired scholar who normally walked almost regally, Pu was bent over as he shuffled forward. He carried a large brass gong, suspended from his neck like a bass drum in a marching band, and struck it with a mallet. The students listened. Over and over, in a subdued, hoarse voice, Pu chanted, "I am a monster!"

The students led Pu and the other teachers in front of the platform, facing the crowd. Just behind and above them, the handsome leader of the Rebels, dressed in an olive drab military uniform, walked to the lectern and began to speak into the microphone. These Spanish teachers, he said in perfect Mandarin, were counterrevolutionaries, monsters who always had opposed the party and Communism. Pu, he charged, was a lackey of anti-Communists and foreigners— he had been an officer in Chiang Kaishek's army and had served as an interpreter for U.S. marines stationed in northern China after World War II. The students pressed nearer to the platform, shaking their fists at the Spanish teachers and shouting slogans: "Long Live Chairman Mao!" "Down with

Monster Pu!" The student leader detailed the charges against each of the Spanish teachers, then paused, feeling the growing fury of the crowd.

"I know there are more monsters!" he yelled. "All the monsters of this school must report to the stage!"

At this signal, the students and young teachers from each department scattered into small groups and shouted out the names of older teachers. The young teachers pointed out some of the semiretired professors, who seldom came to school, and the students ran after them and pushed and pulled them to the platform; other teachers scribbled their colleagues' names on slips of paper and passed them to the Rebels' leader, who read the names into the microphone.

Wen soon was surrounded by a group of frenzied English students. They placed a cap on her head and hung a placard from her neck with a thin piece of wire. The placard read, "Old hag Wen Zengde, bourgeois academic authority," with a red X through her name. One student tied Wen's hands behind her back with straw rope. Then the others pushed her into a line of teachers, all wearing hats and placards, and ordered her to march with them.

Wen was joined by Fang, the department chairman and Chaucer scholar, and Zhu Bingsun, a grammar teacher. The students had run out of paper hats. Zhu was wearing a wastebasket made of willow branches on her head.

Most of the teachers offered little resistance, but several fought back. A few feet away from Wen, a group of young students from the institute's middle school surrounded one of their teachers. She was a tall, thin woman in her late thirties, with a dark complexion, high cheekbones, and long, straight hair. One of the students yanked at her arms, but she fell to the ground and rolled away from them. Another grabbed her legs as she kicked violently. "I am not a monster!" she screamed. Some students kicked back and beat her on the neck and back with their fists while others twisted her arms and tied her up with rope. Then, as she continued to scream, they stood her on her feet and dragged her to the platform.

On the other side of the field, another crowd gathered around a young party official who had been a soldier in the People's Liberation Army. He now was in charge of personnel at the middle school but had been denounced for sexually harassing young women who worked for him. One of them had accused him of attempted rape. The middle school students told him to come with them to the stage. "I am a Communist party member," he replied, and stepped away. "I am from the army, from a poor peasant family."

The students reached for his arms but he fought back. The soldier was short, but unusually broad-shouldered and strong. He threw a series of quick punches and knocked several of them to the ground. Three students jumped on top of him and pushed his face into the dirt while two others tied his hands behind his back. But instead of bringing him to the platform, the students led him to a small tree near the walkway, threw the rope over a branch, and hoisted him off the ground with his hands still tied behind him. The students left him there, screaming and shouting curses, as they rejoined the rally. The cacophony of loud music and chanted slogans drowned out his cries.

By noon, the noise around the field had subsided. The only sound was martial music blaring from the loudspeakers. There were now eighty teachers and school officials lined up in front of the platform, including the heads of all the departments. The music stopped and the Rebels' leader again approached the microphone. "Revolutionary students and teachers!" he yelled. "These are the monsters of our school. Let us have a good look at them."

Then the parade began. A few students pushed their teachers toward the gravel track that ringed the field and began to lead them around it. Other students followed. Soon they had organized a strange march. The eighty teachers shuffled forward as they yelled out their own names. Their hands were tied behind their backs, and their bowed heads were topped by tall hats, wastebaskets, or even spittoons. The students and remaining teachers lined both sides of the track.

At first, the crowd watched this procession almost passively. But as the teachers rounded the track, several students picked up stones from the field and threw them at the teachers. The students from workers' and farmers' families seemed the most upset, as if they were unleashing their anger against the intellectuals who had made them feel inferior. Yet they also seemed to be having fun, as if they were playing a game.

As Wen marched, she chanted "I am a bourgeois academic authority, I am a cow ghost and snake spirit, I am Wen Zengde the monster." One student screamed at her for speaking too softly, then poured a bottle of red ink over her head. It flowed over Wen's face and down her blouse and slacks. Seconds later, she saw another student hurl a bucket of paste at her. The paste splattered over her clothes. A third student poured lime, which was used to patch walls, down her neck and back, stinging her skin.

All around the field, students raced from the classroom buildings with buckets and showered the teachers with torrents of ink and glue. Some students spit in their faces.

The march of teachers slowed as the students ran among them. A few students took off their thick leather belts and strapped the teachers on their backs and legs, demanding that they march faster. Wen bit her tongue as one student thrashed at her and whipped her legs with sharp blows from a metal belt buckle.

Pu and some of the other teachers were forced to the

ground and ordered to crawl over the track. The sharp cinders ripped through Pu's pants and cut his knees. All around her, Wen saw students kicking and spitting at the teachers and striking them with fists, brooms, and brushes. It seemed to go on for hours.

Then the Rebels' leader returned to the platform, apparently satisfied that the teachers had learned their lessons. He announced an end to the rally and called on the school's party secretary, the man who was still nominally in charge of the institute, to comment.

"The Rebels have acted correctly," he said cautiously. "Some of what they did today may have seemed rough, but it is understandable because of their strong class feelings." He told the students to return to their departments. But the Spanish students were not finished with Pu. As the others dispersed, they surrounded him, struck him with their fists, and forced him to crawl out the school's back gate, across the street, and into his apartment building.

As Pu crawled, Wen and the other teachers from the English department were led from the field, across the tree-lined road, and to the front of their redbrick classroom building. They were ordered to kneel on the ground, surrounded by their students and fellow teachers. Lu Guangdan, one of the radical young teachers who had prepared the campaign against Fang, climbed out from a second-floor window and stood on the roof of the portico, yelling down at them through a megaphone.

"I officially announce that you are the monsters of the English department," Lu said. "From today on, you must accept the supervision of the revolutionary masses and confess your crimes."

The students led them into the building and up two flights of stairs to a corner classroom on the third floor. A crude drawing of a ghoul was pasted to the door, over the words

"Monster Corner." The students pushed Wen and the other teachers into the room and ordered them to sit and be silent. Two students stood guard with their arms folded menacingly. One brandished a stick.

The other teachers and students left the building and headed for the cafeteria to eat lunch. Wen and her colleagues, still dripping with ink and paste, sat in the classroom in silence, too shaken and fearful to talk. Hours later, one of the student leaders returned. He threw open the door and glared at them. "Why are you waiting here?" he sneered. "Why don't you go home?"

It was 7 P.M. As Wen approached the back gate, a guard she knew stopped her. He invited her to use the men's room nearby, where she could clean some of the dried ink and paste from her face and clothes. Then, as the sun set, Wen returned to Friendship Village, hoping to avoid anyone she knew.

SEVEN
Shanghai
(November 1966)

 In the days after the August 11 parade, the students at the institute returned to debating among themselves and seemed to lose their interest in attacking the teachers and party officials on campus. At Mao's instruction, they began to organize Red Guard units to spread the revolution throughout the country. Many headed for Beijing, where they would have an opportunity to see Mao in person.

For three months, beginning on August 18, the Shanghai students and more than thirteen million other student revolutionaries from throughout China streamed into the capital to attend rallies. Mao, wearing a Red Guard armband, greeted them from the Gate of Heavenly Peace.[1] The scenes were reminiscent of Hitler's appearances before young fascists at Nuremberg in the 1930s.[2] And this was the image of the Cultural Revolution that the world would remember: millions of fervent young people lined up in Tiananmen Square, wearing red armbands and military uniforms, clutching their little red books, and shouting "Long Live Chairman Mao!"

With classes suspended and no charge for railway transportation, the students also traveled throughout the country to visit other campuses, read wall posters, and discuss the revolution. Some groups of students reenacted parts of the Communists' historic Long March of 1934–35, tramping hundreds of miles into the countryside to spread the revolution to remote villages. For others, the early days of the Cultural Revolution were like a vacation. They traveled for free to historic or scenic sites, visited friends and relatives, and took advantage of free food and shelter at schools and colleges along the way.[3]

On city streets, the students attacked anything and anyone they linked with the "four olds"—old ideas, old customs, old culture, and old habits. Red Guards stopped people who wore tight pants and slashed their clothes with knives or scissors. They cut the hair off girls who wore long or fashionable hairdos, sometimes shaving all the hair from one side of their heads to imitate the "yin-yang" haircut once used to punish prostitutes. On buses, the Guards led recitations of Mao's quotations and beat people who were not carrying the little red book or wearing a badge with Chairman Mao's picture.[4]

Students covered windows and walls with big-character posters and portraits of Mao. They tore down shop signs and street signs with old-fashioned names. (For example, Prosperity Road became Antirevisionist Street; overnight, hundreds of stores formerly named "Fortune" and "Lucky" changed their names to "East Is Red" and "Revolution.") In the middle of Nanjing Road in Shanghai, the busiest shopping district in all of China, a giant red banner hung opposite the Number One Department Store. The white lettering read: "Long Live the Red Terror!"[5]

The Red Guards burned books, destroyed temples and monuments, and even dug up family cemeteries to rob coffins of gold and jewelry. They broke into the homes of wealthy intellectuals and party officials to steal their goods; they beat those who resisted. Rival factions of Guards, and visiting Guards from different cities, often would search one home again and again, occasionally showing up at the same time.[6] That fall, different groups of Red Guards searched Wen Zengde's house three times, stealing her clothes, jewelry, and antiques and sealing off her study with strips of paper.

But by late September Mao and his supporters had recognized that the student revolutionaries were attacking the wrong targets, focusing too much on the "four olds" and failing to criticize conservative party officials. The Red Guards were dominated by students from cadre and military families, who had tried to limit the attacks on party leaders. The most radical revolutionaries—students from middle-class and intellectual families who had suffered from the party's and work teams' emphasis on class background— were at first excluded from Red Guard membership. These bourgeois students went to extremes to prove their revolutionary loyalty. That fall, Mao recognized their importance and, for the first time, permitted the students from "bad" class backgrounds to become members of the Red Guards. He encouraged all of the students to attack more serious targets. Mao had radicalized the Cultural Revolution; the deep class divisions and vague goals would lead to even further violence.[7]

Students and young teachers at the Shanghai Foreign Languages Institute began arresting party officials and others suspected of opposing the revolution. Early in November, a Red Guard came to arrest Wen. He took her to the institute and locked her in a small, dark room in the women's dormitory.

Wen woke up early on her first day as a prisoner. A group of Red Guards had come to take her to a different room.

They helped her collect her belongings and walked with her across the sports field and into the English department building. Then they locked her inside a familiar room on the third floor. It was a large classroom near the teachers' reference room, where Wen had once taught conversation to first-year students. The windows were now barred. Wen laid down her straw bedding on two long, flat school desks that had been pushed together and hung her mosquito net from a hook in the ceiling. Other desks and chairs were scattered about the room—the legs had been broken off several of the chairs—and there was a bucket in the corner to serve as a toilet.

At noon, a Guard unlocked the door and told Wen it was time for lunch. She followed him outside to the front of the building. There were about thirty people waiting there. Wen knew most of them, the older English teachers who had been criticized in the poster campaigns earlier that summer and fall. But she was surprised to see some party and school officials, like Wang Jiyu, the school's vice president. The Guards lined them up in single file and ordered them to remain silent. Then the group walked toward the dining hall with their heads down. At the front of the line, one of the Guards carried a pike and tassel, similar to the ones used to lead prisoners to their executions.

As they walked, Wen saw other lines of prisoners emerging from the buildings around campus. A group of Spanish teachers marched from the audiovisual building behind the sports field. Some Russian teachers walked from the other end of the redbrick building attached to the English department. Wen had trouble keeping her head down. From all ends of the campus, she saw school administrators, older teachers, and party officials from every department marching in line, surrounded by Red Guards who sang revolutionary songs and shoved prisoners who strayed back into formation.

The scene would be repeated three times a day, at breakfast, lunch, and dinner. By the time she reached the dining hall, Wen had counted more than two hundred prisoners. Inside, she queued up at the windows to buy her rice and vegetables, not daring to talk to anyone. Then the guards led another march away from the dining hall. Wen returned to her locked classroom prison to eat her lunch.

That night after dinner, at about 8:30, Wen heard a key turning in the lock of her door. Two Red Guards entered, and one told her it was time for an interrogation session.

The interrogation room was past the reference room, at the other end of the third floor. This also had been a classroom. Desks and broken chairs were scattered against the walls. Five Red Guards stood in the middle of the room and circled around Wen after she was led in. The Guards disguised their identities with handkerchiefs or white surgical masks over their faces. Wen was sure she didn't know any of them. She guessed from their accents that they were from just north of Shanghai.

One of the girls started the questioning. She barked out her words as she glared at Wen, gesturing by waving a sandalwood fan.

"Wen Zengde. You are a bourgeois ideologist. Why were you born in America?"

Wen was too baffled by the question to answer. When she hesitated, the girl struck Wen across the face with the fan. A boy yelled another question at her.

"Why did you spy for the Nationalists?"

Again, Wen failed to answer. He picked up one of the broken chair legs from the floor and hit Wen hard on the back of her thigh. He asked another question.

"Why did you send secret materials to your counterrevolutionary husband in Hong Kong?"

Wen could not remain silent.

"I did not send any secret materials to my husband."

Her response seemed to anger all of them. One tied her hands behind her back with straw rope, then attached the rope to a pulley on the ceiling. Another then pushed her to the floor, where she kneeled on some thick rope. The coarse rope cut through her pants and jabbed at her knees.

The Guards repeated their accusation over and over, demanding that Wen confess to sending secrets to Hong Kong. Each time she refused, they pulled the rope attached to her hands toward the ceiling, lifting her arms behind her back. She gritted her teeth—her arm and back muscles tore and twisted as the rope lifted her off the floor and cut into her wrists. After a few seconds in the air, one of the Guards let go of the rope. Wen smashed to the floor, landing hard on the pile of rope, which stabbed her knees.

The Guards seemed to enjoy this torture of a sixty-seven-year-old woman. Wen thought she heard the girl laugh as she hit the floor. They lifted her off the floor perhaps a dozen times.

"Are you ready to confess to your crimes, to sending secrets to Hong Kong?"

"I did not send any secrets."

Then the Guards began to beat her with the chair legs again, bruising her shins and thighs. They stopped for a few seconds and demanded her confession. But Wen gave them the same answer each time and got the same response from them—a torrent of blows.

After an hour of this, Wen heard two of the boys talking in a corner of the room. She felt they looked tired from all the effort they had exerted.

"This old hag must be insane," one of them said. "After all these beatings, she has not shed a tear or yelled out."

But Wen was determined not to give them any satisfaction for their cruelty. She had made up her mind to withstand the beating and torture without making a sound; she would not act weak or ask for mercy. She would endure.

Although it officially had been outlawed by the Communist government, torture had long been an established part of the Chinese legal system. The Chinese penal code was developed in 650, during the Tang dynasty. Defendants were forced to kneel before judges on a stone floor, sometimes with thin chains under their knees. Judges were permitted to question defendants under torture if they had sufficient proof of guilt.[8]

Legal methods of torture included flogging, beating the back of the thighs with bamboo sticks, applying screws to hands and ankles, and slapping the face with leather flaps. One of the fundamental rules of the penal code was that no one could be sentenced until he confessed to his crime.[9]

But the Communists developed a far more sophisticated system for dealing with persons they considered criminals. It used psychology, Chinese tradition, and Communist methods and doctrine. It was designed not simply to punish so-called criminals but to reform them. In the West, it is commonly referred to as "brainwashing."[10]

The Communists developed this method to help win over those Chinese, particularly intellectuals, who had been Nationalist supporters. The goal was to convince them that the old ways were poisonous and reform would make them part of the new society. It borrowed the element of confession from the Chinese penal system, but added a Communist focus on reeducation.[11]

In its use in reeducation centers in the early 1950s, this remolding system worked by isolating individuals and using group pressure to make people feel a sense of guilt for their old ways and beliefs. Public self-criticism provided a chance to confess past sins and promise to become a new person.

Those who failed to repent were denounced at public struggle sessions. Even the most virtuous individual was made to blame himself for the suffering imposed by the group and to convince himself he needed to reform.[12]

The Red Guards and others used similar tactics during the Cultural Revolution, although their techniques were generally less sophisticated. But even without the isolation of a walled prison or reeducation center, they could compel people to feel guilt and to criticize themselves. The closely supervised work units and neighborhoods, which provided a sense of community in calmer times, became a source of unrelenting pressure during the Cultural Revolution. It became a test of loyalty for every work unit, neighborhood, and family to criticize people who were singled out. Those who joined in were rewarded; those who resisted were singled out themselves.

But these pressures had less influence on Wen Zengde. She had been raised in a society that cherished individualism and personal freedom. She felt betrayed, not guilty, when her friends, neighbors, and colleagues attacked her.

After a few days of captivity, Wen had settled into a routine. She had rice porridge and steamed bread for breakfast, rice and vegetables for lunch, perhaps some pork for dinner. On some mornings, there were struggle sessions in the auditorium where the Red Guards publicly taunted a group of teachers or officials. But on most mornings and afternoons Wen studied Chairman Mao's works, mended clothes for the Red Guards, and wrote detailed answers to their accusations against her.

Even the evening torture became routine. Each night at 8:30, the Red Guards took her to the interrogation room. The questions and answers were always the same. They persisted in charging that she had spied for her husband;

Wen refused to confess. Only the torture and the threats changed. On some nights they kicked her with their thick-soled shoes or hit her with belt buckles and chair legs. One of the Guards seemed to take pleasure in giving her a "handshake," squeezing her hands so hard that it felt as if her bones were breaking. Wen was most afraid of their threats. One Red Guard who was angered by her answers threatened to cut out her tongue.

The Guards seemed fanatical and cruel, but Wen recognized a careful calculation in their actions. They rarely struck her above the clothing line, avoiding her hands, face, and neck. And even when they appeared to be in a frenzy of beating, kicking, and swearing, they would suddenly stop, as if they had received a signal, and let her go for the night. Wen felt that someone, perhaps one of the young teachers, was directing their actions. When she returned to her room each night, Wen scratched a nail on the windowsill to mark another day in captivity.

On the tenth day of her imprisonment, the Guards called on Wen in the afternoon and took her to another classroom in the English department. Five of the radical young teachers were there, sitting behind a long table like a panel of judges. Wen knew them well. They all had been her students when she first started teaching at the institute, and she had trained them to teach English. Since the Cultural Revolution began, they all had taken an active role—some were from the group that had prepared the poster campaign against the head of the English department and had helped the Red Guards pick out teachers to be paraded in the rally on the sports field.

They motioned for the Red Guards to leave the room and looked disapprovingly at Wen. A stack of Wen's English conversation materials was piled on the table in front of them. Wang Changrong—whom Wen had embarrassed by criticizing his flawed conversation dialogues—spoke first.

"This conversation here," he said, opening a pamphlet to an exercise about shopping in a department store. "It is full of poisonous words. You have a woman asking for vanishing cream. This is ridiculous. No proletarian uses such bourgeois things."

Wen listened without responding.

"At the end of the shopping," Hou Weirui said, "the clerk takes the girl's money, wraps up the package, then says: 'Goodbye. Come again.' This is a poisonous weed, the words of a capitalist society. Socialists would never talk this way. Why would we ask someone to 'Come again'? That is bourgeois talk."

"And this word 'beautiful,'" Wang added. "This is the word of a capitalist. You must say 'healthy,' not 'beautiful.'"

They also ridiculed Wen's dialogue on foreign table manners, criticizing her for explaining how to eat soup and how to use a knife and fork.

"You are a wicked old woman," Hou said, "trying to poison students by teaching them the bourgeois life-style."

The young teachers demanded that Wen write a self-criticism of her bourgeois ideology and post it in the department. That night, when the Red Guards beat her, they asked Wen if she had finished her self-criticism.

Wen wrote it on newsprint the next morning. She admitted that she had failed to use proletarian language. Shi Songchuan, a young teacher who had been under attack himself, came with a Red Guard to pick it up. Shi helped Wen add some punctuation, then said he would paste up the criticism himself.

The young teachers and Red Guards seemed pleased with Wen's criticism. By the next day, they had covered the department walls with attacks on Wen. But the beatings each night continued.

* * *

Many of the suicides—or murders that were covered up by calling them suicides—occurred as a result of such torture.

Song Yongqing, the brilliant young English teacher, was the first from the Foreign Languages Institute to commit suicide. Later that summer, after the Red Guards took power at the school, two teachers in the Russian department killed themselves. One escaped from an interrogation session on the fourth floor of the building connected to the English department and leapt from a window, smashing his head on a walkway that was lined with big-character posters. Another Russian teacher electrocuted himself by sticking his finger in a light fixture at his home when he was about to be interrogated.

The Red Guards also imprisoned and tortured school employees whose loyalty they questioned. A man who worked in the English department print shop was detained in the summer of 1966 because he had once been a student at a Nationalist intelligence school. His record had been cleared in the 1950s, however, and he had married and had three young children. But during the Cultural Revolution his past arose to haunt him. The Red Guards organized a struggle session in the English department, and his neighbors and his children's teachers yelled insults and curses at him for hours as he knelt in front of them. When everyone had left the room, the printer stood up, walked to a window, and leapt to his death.

One of Wen's earliest friends in Shanghai also committed suicide that summer. Her name was Zhang Shen, and she had befriended—as well as spied on—Wen after Wen arrived at the Shanghai First Teachers' College. They had taught together for two years, but Zhang remained with the teachers' college when Wen's department was transferred to the institute.

At the beginning of the Cultural Revolution, the Red

Guards at the teachers' college interrogated Zhang about her links with the United States. (She had worked for the YWCA in China, which had sent her to the United States to study before 1949.) But the Guards' questioning was mild compared with the torture she suffered at home. Her husband, a dietitian at the Number One Medical College, had left home to live with his mistress, a nurse at the college. Zhang's eldest son, a fanatical Red Guard, forced his mother to crawl along the floor as he and his friends stood on her back. After several days, Zhang was unable to stand up. Her backbone had been fractured. Doctors at the local hospitals refused to treat her because she was accused of being a spy. Her son continued to torture her, forcing her to crawl around the neighborhood and recite quotations from Mao.

When Wen heard of Zhang's suffering, she visited her at home. Zhang's spirit, as well as her back, had been broken.

"Don't educate your children!" Zhang yelled at Wen. She started to cry. Wen tried to assure her that education was not the cause of her suffering, but Zhang just shook her head and sent Wen away. A few days later, Zhang left a note on the kitchen table and crawled out of her house. The note said that the bus driver should not be blamed for her death. Zhang threw herself under the wheels of a trolley bus and was crushed to death.

A few years after the Cultural Revolution ended, the school held a memorial service for Zhang. Her son read a long eulogy praising his mother. "I can still see her face beaming toward us," her son said. Few of the teachers present were able to hide their contempt for his hypocrisy.

Amid all the cruelty, there were moments of kindness.

One Red Guard, indistinguishable from the others except for his gentle voice, seemed eager to help Wen when he could. Twice, he escorted Shen Yanping, the daughter of

Wen's housemaid, into Wen's room. The girl, who also wore a Red Guard uniform, brought Wen soup, duck, and eggs. But the real comfort was to know that someone on the outside still cared about her.

About five weeks after Wen had been taken prisoner, the Red Guard with the gentle voice performed another good deed. He brought Wen two thermoses from her home. He had filled them with hot water.

"Here, now you can take a bath," he said. "Just let me know when you begin so I can watch the door."

That night, after she returned from hours of questioning and beating, Wen nodded to him as he closed her door. She took off her torn and dusty clothes and poured the hot water in her washbasin. In the weak fluorescent light, Wen could see the damage that had been done to her body in those five weeks. Nearly all of her flesh was red or purple with scars and bruises. Some of the blows had broken the skin and left clots of blood. Wen stepped in the basin and rubbed the hot water over her legs, thinking of her gratitude to the young man with the sweet voice.

EIGHT
Shanghai
(August 1968)

 Wen Zengde learned about the workers' arrival early that morning when she heard the firecrackers, gongs, and drums from the parade that welcomed them. But she couldn't see much from her padlocked room in the women's dormitory.

The students and teachers at the Foreign Languages Institute had hung a huge banner over the top of the school's iron gate: "We Welcome Mao Zedong's Thought Propaganda Team to Our Institute to Exercise Leadership." The walls beside the gate and the makeshift bulletin boards that lined the main road through campus were covered by hundreds of posters, pledging loyalty to the team.

At 9 A.M., the institute's students and teachers—except for those, like Wen, who remained imprisoned—crowded into the school auditorium. A handful of Red Guards in their familiar uniforms were at the front of the room, but most of the stage was occupied by more than a hundred factory workers. They were much older than the students, and their dress was distinctly different. They wore heavy boots, blue pants, and white or blue shirts. A huge Mao button was pinned to each of their shirts, and they wore red armbands identifying them as propaganda team members. Most of them also carried red cloth bags, with a crude embroidery of Mao's profile, slung over their shoulders. They wore blue steelworkers' caps, which had unusually long bills to protect them from the sparks and heat of the steel furnaces.

A Red Guard leader from the French department introduced the workers. Then a tall man in his mid-thirties took over the microphone.

"We are the workers from the Number Three Steel Plant," he said in Mandarin Chinese, with a strong Shanghai accent. "We are the new leaders of your school. We are prepared to make sacrifices to carry out Chairman Mao's revolutionary line."

Some of the teachers were frightened by his tough talk. He was suggesting that the workers, traditionally hostile to intellectuals, were prepared, if necessary, to give up their lives if the students and teachers tried to undermine them.

"We know we are not welcome here," the workers' leader continued, "even though you have pledged support and put up signs. The intellectuals have never accepted working-class leadership. But now, for the first time, the proletariat has taken control. This is a historic event."

At the end of the speech, members of each department returned to their offices to meet with the workers assigned to supervise them. Dozens of workers met with the English teachers in the teachers' reference room. They announced plans to organize the department militarily, with companies and platoons. The company commander for the English department, a very tall man in his mid-twenties, spoke to them in Shanghai dialect. He was coarse and direct.

"We are on guard against sabotage from class enemies,"

he said. "We represent the whole working class. The Cultural Revolution will carry on, and we will be the leading group."

The company commander told them there would be exercise and marching every morning and political-study sessions all day and three nights a week. There would be no time to relax. The workers, he said, would begin meeting with individual teachers, visiting their homes, and examining their backgrounds. The English teachers applauded him, even his threats.

In the months since Wen first was imprisoned and beaten, the Cultural Revolution had descended into chaos. The Red Guards had returned from their travels around the country and, led by hyperradical students from bourgeois and intellectual families, were encouraged to form organizations that challenged party leadership. In Shanghai, the Red Guards had virtually overthrown the municipal government.

The students helped form a radical workers' group that opposed the mayor. Nie Yuanzi from Beijing University, whose big-character poster had inspired campus rebellions at the beginning of the Cultural Revolution, came to Shanghai to criticize the head of the city education department and the mayor. Radicals took control of a Shanghai newspaper to demand that it publish Nie's remarks. Conservative groups battled with the radicals and, after eight conservatives reportedly were killed, called for a general strike. The city government resigned several days later, and the city's banks, electrical system, and transportation shut down. With Mao's support, the radicals took over political and administrative control of Shanghai. Radicals throughout China were urged to take similar actions, and violence spread.[1]

Attempts by the military to control the radicals brought the nation to the brink of civil war.[2] Radicals in Wuhan and other cities seized weapons from armories and battled with conservatives. The radicals' actions were encouraged by Mao's wife, Jiang Qing, who urged them to "attack with words, defend with force." In Beijing, they assaulted foreign diplomats and burned down the British legation.[3]

Violence at Qinghua University in Beijing finally forced Mao to take action against the Red Guards. He ordered in troops and repudiated the students, calling for "worker-peasant Mao Zedong Thought propaganda teams," with the help of the military, to take over the universities. His supporters argued that the bourgeois outlook of the radical students had led to anarchy; it was time for the working class to take power. The Red Guards were demobilized.[4]

While the Red Guards were in control, Wen had been held in a small room in the women's dormitory. She was allowed to leave only for meals and criticism sessions before her department. At night, Guards would try to force her to confess. When she heard the announcements as the workers paraded onto the Foreign Languages Institute campus, Wen hoped she would be set free.

The night the workers arrived, the students came to Wen's room for a final visit. Two of them tied her hands behind her back with straw rope. A girl, about nineteen, who seemed to be their leader, told Wen they were taking her "to the gallows." She strung a long rope through a hook on the ceiling, then tied a noose around Wen's neck. The girl slowly pulled on the rope until Wen's feet dangled in the air. Wen held her breath as the noose dug into her throat.

"You have sent secret materials to your husband in Hong Kong, a Nationalist agent!" the girl yelled. "If you confess your guilt, we will let you down at once."

Wen tried to shake her head, and they lowered her to the ground. She repeated the reply she had been making for months.

"I do not have any place to obtain any secret materials," Wen said. "What proof do you have that I was given such materials?"

The girl pulled hard on the rope and lifted Wen off the floor again. She gasped for air.

"You have telegraphed the materials to your husband," the girl said. "Confess now and we will be lenient."

Wen caught her breath as they let her down a second time, but she remained defiant.

"Have you checked with the telegraph office?" Wen asked. "Do they have any records that I sent a message to a foreign country?" Wen insisted on asking the logical questions, even in the face of madness.

The torture continued for an hour. Each time Wen shook her head or questioned them, the students grew angrier and pulled her off the floor. Finally, Wen lost consciousness and collapsed. The students, in a final effort to prove their worth to the school's new leaders and Chairman Mao, could not force Wen to confess to crimes she hadn't committed. After they left, Wen crawled to her straw mat in the corner to sleep.

For the next few days, the students seemed distracted, paying less attention to Wen and the other prisoners. At night, when the students usually came to beat her and demand her confession, Wen was left alone. Perhaps, she thought, her hopes about the school's new leaders were correct. The summer heat was dissipating and the early fall, the most pleasant season in Shanghai, would begin soon.

About a week after the workers arrived, Wen was summoned to a 10 A.M. meeting in the English department. When she got there, the room already was filled with students and young teachers. One of the students led her to the front of the room. Wen realized this meeting was for her. It was a struggle session.

The struggle session was one of the main weapons of the

Cultural Revolution. Its purpose was to break the will to resist, to humiliate a victim in front of—and with the active help of—friends, colleagues, and family. Some struggle sessions against high-ranking intellectuals took place in huge stadiums, with thousands of people joining in. Sometimes the victims would be beaten and verbally attacked for hours as onlookers jeered and yelled insults.[5] But the goal of the struggle session was not simply to humiliate or force confessions. It also was a way to force everyone to participate in the excesses of the revolution, to make them share responsibility.

Most of the sessions were like the one Wen now faced, a small gathering of fellow teachers, former students, and friends. Wen knew how to act. She faced the crowd, stood at attention with her hands by her sides and her feet close together, and lowered her head. She could not see her accusers.

"You came to China as a traitor, a spy pretending to be an English teacher!" one of them yelled at her. "Now reveal what you have done!"

"I am not a traitor," Wen said. "I came only to teach English."

Dozens of voices yelled at her in unison: "A liar! A liar!"

Wen recognized many of the voices. Some had been her friends, others once had been her students and now were young teachers. Although a few were driven by ambition, most joined in out of fear, echoing the lies of their colleagues in order to protect themselves.

"Where did you hide the spyglass, the wireless receiver, and other instruments for spying?" another voice asked, repeating the accusations she had been hearing from the Red Guards who tortured her.

Wen repeated her response, almost by rote. It would have been impossible for her to smuggle such items through customs, she said, because they carefully searched all her bags at Shenzhen when she arrived from Hong Kong in 1956.

The chant from the department was the same: "A liar! A liar!"

"Why did you send secret materials to your counterrevolutionary husband in Hong Kong? How many times have you telegraphed him?"

Teachers and students repeated the accusations again and again, until Wen stopped answering.

"Are you afraid of leaking out your secret?" another voice asked.

Wen stood immobile. After two hours, the questions and taunts stopped. A worker untied Wen's hands as her colleagues left the room and headed for the cafeteria for lunch.

Over the next few weeks, the struggle sessions against Wen and her colleagues became more frequent. A few days after her first session, Wen was led to the library again. For a moment, she stood there alone, steeling herself for another assault of questions and insults. But this session was not for her.

She turned to see her colleague, Zhu Bingsun, being led into the library. Zhu, wearing a placard around her neck, bowed her head as the teachers and students pushed her onto the platform beside Wen.

She had known Zhu for nearly ten years, but her colleague remained an enigma. Perhaps it was Zhu's acting background or her desire to conceal secrets from her past, but Wen never could be sure when Zhu was telling the truth.

Zhu liked to tell stories of growing up in the 1920s in Beijing. Zhu said she lived for a time in the home of Pan Fu, the Chinese prime minister in 1927–28, where her stepmother tutored Pan's children. It was there, Zhu said, that she fell in love with Beijing opera, watching some of the great actors of the day perform for Pan's guests. Wen was skeptical of those stories. She had lived in Beijing in those days, too, and some of what Zhu said seemed exaggerated.

Like Wen, Zhu attended Yenching University. But in her second year, Zhu said, she left school to join a traveling Beijing opera troupe. Her stepmother forced her to return to school after she missed one semester.

Zhu studied German literature in college and, at about the time Germany was invading eastern Europe, she took a job as a translator at the German embassy in Beijing. Years later, Zhu told her colleagues that she spent most of her time taking the wives of visiting German businessmen on tours of the city. But some of the teachers at the institute wondered whether, in this instance, Zhu had understated her role.

After the war, Zhu worked for the Nationalists as an interpreter and typist in the Foreign Affairs Office. Zhu said she spent most of her evenings attending dancing parties and banquets with British and U.S. diplomats. On the last day of 1945, she married the head of the Foreign Affairs Office. He died during the civil war with the Communists.

One rumor about Zhu was that her husband had left her a fortune, which she had used to bribe officials during the Cultural Revolution. Wen and the others at the institute didn't know what to make of Zhu's other stories about her love life. Zhu told some of her friends that she had been married two more times after her first husband died. One man was reportedly an actor whom she divorced after two years, another a poet she had met in line at a movie theater and married the same day. She rarely mentioned her fourth husband, a petty thief who was sent to prison during the Cultural Revolution.

Zhu also said little about her two sons. The elder, from her first marriage, was a cook; the younger son was a factory worker. Both had been active Red Guards who had joined in criticism sessions against their mother.

As Zhu was pushed to the front of the department meeting, Wen looked at her with some admiration. Zhu was a convincing actress, Wen thought, playing the role of the unjustly accused prisoner. Her clothes were torn and patched, her face was smeared with dirt, and her hair was disheveled.

"Down with the traitor Zhu Bingsun!" the crowd yelled at her. Zhu stood quietly beside Wen, her head bowed. The screams echoed in Wen's ears.

"What were you doing at the German embassy? What were you typing?"

"Why were you married to the Nationalist leader? Why did you have so many husbands?"

Like Song Yongqing, who was denounced initially for leaving his fiancée and dating a student, Zhu's morality was under examination. But Zhu simply nodded at whatever anyone yelled. After two hours, the questions, accusations, and taunts ended. It was time for lunch. The struggle sessions had become almost a banal routine, a form of entertainment to break up the day.

The department was not yet finished with Zhu. After lunch, a group of students led her outside to be paraded around campus. As Wen watched from her locked room, the students attached posters to her front and back that accused her of being the wife of a Nationalist leader and an enemy of the people. Zhu's appearance seemed almost comic, reminding Wen of the men wearing sandwich boards she had seen in her youth in San Francisco. Zhu also wore a tall hat that read "Zhu Bingsun, Traitor." A red X crossed out her name. She carried a cymbal and a wooden mallet as she was led around campus yelling: "I am Zhu Bingsun, traitor and enemy of the people." It was like the parade Zhu and Wen had marched in two years earlier.

A group of middle school students joined in. As Zhu crossed the campus, the youngsters spat at her and picked up stones and threw them at her. They continued to follow her out the back gate toward her home. When Zhu reached her apartment, Wen learned later, her older son and her neighbors also began to chant her crimes and throw stones at her as she was led through the neighborhood in her strange costume. Zhu's son followed her, beating her with a stick.

At the institute, Zhu had survived the suffering and humiliation by seeing herself as an actress playing a role. But at home, with her neighbors and son turning against her, she was no longer acting. The pain was real.

That evening, Zhu collected four small bottles of DDT. The neighborhood association had continued to distribute the insecticide during the summer months, even when it was widely known that victims of the Cultural Revolution had been drinking it to commit suicide. Then she wrote a note to her younger son, telling him where she kept her money and asking him to let her sleep late the next morning. Zhu drank the DDT quickly—it burned her throat as she swallowed— and went to bed.

Back at the institute, three students came to visit Wen in her room that night, but they didn't bring rope with them.

"What education did you get from today's struggle session?" one of them asked.

"I was educated to differentiate between right and wrong," Wen replied, "to differentiate between the enemies and ourselves."

"This old hag teacher got some education!" the youngest one said. The three of them laughed loudly and left.

The DDT was not enough to kill Zhu. When her younger son found her in bed the next morning, he ran to get a doctor who lived next door. They took her to a nearby hospital, but the staff at first refused to treat her because they considered Zhu a counterrevolutionary. Many victims of the revolution died because they could not get medical treatment. The doctor had good connections, however, and got her admitted. After six days, Zhu recovered and returned home. Some months later, she would try to kill herself again.

The struggle sessions continued for the other teachers, unaffected by Zhu's suicide attempt. The day she went to the hospital, a meeting for the entire school was held in the auditorium. Wen and all the imprisoned teachers from each department were lined up in the back of the room.

At 1 P.M., the students led three women into the auditorium. Wen recognized two of them: one worked in the treasury department, and the other was Jiang Zejiu, a colleague from the English department. They all wore placards and tall hats. The auditorium was filled with workers, students, and teachers.

Jiang, who was in her forties, had been a Catholic nun before the Communist victory in 1949. But since then she had been an English teacher, one of the most respected and well-liked teachers at the school. She stood silently, her head bowed, as her former friends and students yelled at her. They made fun of her for her practice of plucking her eyebrows and ridiculed her religious background.

"How did you marry Jesus?" one asked. "He has so many thousands of wives."

"Why did you come here to earn money and eat grain the peasants grow? Why not get it from your God?"

One student standing near her on the stage grabbed her from behind by the hair, pulling her head back.

"This is what the face of a nun looks like!" he yelled.

Hers was not a political crime, Wen thought, it was a matter of religion. Why did they single her out?

As the winter months approached, propaganda teams throughout the country had succeeded in restoring order, sometimes with the help of the army. Under Mao's directive, millions of students were sent from cities into the countryside to be reeducated by the peasants. Mao also had reorganized the revolutionary committees in the provinces, concentrating power in the hands of the military. The next step was to reorganize the Communist party, officially expelling Liu Shaoqi and setting the stage for army chief Lin Biao to become Mao's officially designated successor.[6] The revolution could now focus on Mao's May 1968 directive to "purify class ranks." His goal was to purge radical leftists, but the local committees cast a much wider net.[7]

The worker-peasant propaganda teams were particularly well suited to purifying class ranks. At first, the teams at the institute held frequent struggle sessions and ordered the older teachers who had been imprisoned by the Red Guards to write confessions and self-criticisms. But the workers and soldiers had far more power and authority than the students. They had access to the professors' and cadres' files, the secret dossiers that the party kept on every adult in China.[8] The files held information about friends and family background, complaints, rumors, and personnel department reports. Some files even included pages of diaries that others had submitted.

The propaganda teams met secretly with some of the young teachers to investigate the files. A few of the teachers and workers traveled around the country to collect additional information.

These young teachers were the same ambitious, loyal party members (mostly from working-class families, like Wang, Hou, and Lu) who two years earlier had assisted the Red Guards in identifying the "monsters" in their midst. Their skills at scheming and manipulation had served them well. Now they were helping the propaganda teams reach a final judgment against all of their colleagues. The team in each department posted the names of faculty and cadres who were under suspicion. The other teachers were expected to volunteer information about them.

The first list in the English department consisted of the names of older teachers who had been held by the Red Guards, along with those of some middle-aged teachers who so far had been left alone. Some of them had been respected party members and officials. The list included Li Guanyi, who had studied at Stanford in the 1950s and was now labeled an American spy; Yang Xiaoshi, the department vice chairman, who had a Swiss mother and had taught in a Nationalist military medical college; Wang Jiyu, the school vice president who had been an active Communist in the early 1930s and was president of Harbin University until she was criticized in the Anti-Rightist campaign; Jiang Zejiu, the former nun; Zhang Peicheng, a former acting president of the school who had studied in the Soviet Union in the 1930s but was now held in a Shanghai prison and accused of being a Soviet spy; Qin Xiaomeng, a former department vice chairman whose husband, once a Nationalist officer, had surrendered to the Communists during the civil war; Zhu Bingsun; and Wen Zengde.

All teachers and staff who had not been imprisoned gathered each morning at six o'clock for exercise. Then they marched in formation—or as close to a formation as college teachers could manage—on the sports field. The rest of the day was taken up with political-study sessions. The teachers, closely supervised by the workers from their platoon, read and recited Chairman Mao's works, as well as the writings of Marx, Engels, and Lenin and editorials in the *People's Daily*. During their discussions, the teachers mostly parroted the works they were studying. They knew anything they said that didn't comply with current policy would be reported to the authorities. The workers, many of whom were barely literate, often led the study sessions. Whenever a worker read from Mao's works, the teachers heaped praise on him, regardless of how poorly he read.

The teachers had little chance to get to know the individual workers. The members of the propaganda team changed frequently, with new workers from the steel plant arriving every few weeks. Departments held farewell parties for workers who returned to the plant. At one of those parties, sponsored by the middle school affiliated with the institute, a teacher boldly asked one of the departing workers to return the money she had borrowed. Other teachers at the party then complained that they, too, had lent money to the same worker. But the money never was returned, and the teachers didn't dare press the issue.

The teachers heard other stories about unscrupulous workers. One woman on the propaganda team, for example, had been cited as a model worker. She was rewarded for continuing her duties at the school even after she learned her husband had been hospitalized with a fatal illness. But the teachers later found out the real reason that the woman didn't visit her dying husband. She had been having an affair with an army official assigned to the institute's propaganda team. After several team members caught them making love in a dormitory room, the woman and the officer were quietly removed from the team and sent back to their work units.

For most of the workers, the time at the institute seemed like a vacation. They also made sure that the staff at the school didn't have to work hard, either. So the menial jobs—cleaning toilets, sweeping the floors, working in the kitchens, taking care of the grounds—were assigned to the school's teachers. The workers often laughed at the sight of the once-proud intellectuals carrying mops instead of books.

Wen had been writing "self-criticisms" almost since the day the propaganda team arrived. She had written hundreds of pages, responding to what she had seen at struggle sessions or read in Mao's works. But the propaganda team wasn't interested in Wen's writing. They wanted her to confess her crimes.

Wen continued to keep track of the days. It was winter now, and the Chinese New Year was approaching. But Wen was a prisoner without a sentence, with no idea when she would be set free. It had been more than five months—she had made 160 scratches on her wall with a nail—since the arrival of the workers had lifted her hopes and more than two years since she first was imprisoned.

That night, after she returned from dinner, Wen heard a key in the padlock of her room. A student and a worker from the propaganda team threw open the door. The worker spat out his brief speech to her.

"All of your self-criticisms are unacceptable," he said. "They are only stories for a three-year-old child to read or to believe. You do not realize the seriousness of your crimes. Therefore, we are taking you to another room to be confined. Pick up your things right away and come with us!"

Wen felt angry but she remained silent. She quietly followed them on a short walk to the audiovisual building, where the broadcast station was located and the Red Guards had once had their headquarters. They led her to the third floor and into a small room. It looked like a storage closet.

The worker looked at Wen sternly. "When you confess your crimes," he said, "you will be taken to a better room." He locked the door and left with the student.

The room was dark and Wen reached for the light bulb overhead. In the weak light, she could see that the room had no windows or furniture. The only thing with her in the room was a metal bucket that was to be her toilet. Wen knelt down and laid out her straw mat. It was too big for the room. When she stretched out, Wen, who was less than five feet tall, found that her feet and head touched the walls. She bent her knees toward her chest and tried to sleep.

Early the next day, Wen heard the door being unlocked. But there was no one in the hall by the time she got up. She walked down the hall to the bathroom to empty her bucket and wash her face. She could see the early morning sunlight through the bathroom window and knew another day had begun. Her neck and back were stiff. Wen missed her room in the dormitory.

One of the workers was waiting in the hall to lead her to the dining hall for breakfast. On the stairway, they joined four other women prisoners. Wen recognized Wang Jiyu, the former vice president of the institute. She seemed to have suffered badly. Wang clung to the handrail with both hands as they walked down the stairs.

A group of students and workers, carrying pikes and tassels and singing revolutionary songs, led them to join the other prisoners on their way to breakfast. Wang could barely walk. On the way back that morning, Wen tried to help her to her room. Wang's back was so twisted that she could only crawl up the stairs. When Wen got to her own room, one of the workers handed her some rice paper and a fountain pen and told her to write another self-criticism. Wen sat against the wall with her knees bent and tried to write with the paper against her legs.

Late that night, sometime after midnight, a student unlocked the door and led Wen out of the building toward the English department. It was raining heavily as they walked across campus, and the rain soaked through Wen's clothes. She clutched her self-criticism close to her, trying to keep the ink from running.

Wen thought she might be going to another struggle session, but the uncertainty frightened her. The student led her to a big room on the first floor of the redbrick English building. The room was a brightly lit classroom thick with smoke and the smell of liquor. Four workers, all dressed in blue pants and white shirts, sat behind a long table facing the door. The student motioned for Wen to sit on a wooden chair opposite the table, then sat down near her.

Wen thought the workers looked drunk. The oldest man, about fifty, with bushy eyebrows, appeared to be in charge. He scowled at Wen and told her they wanted her to write a complete autobiography. The workers stared at her for a few minutes, then the older man waved the back of his hand to signal the student to take Wen back to her room.

For the next two weeks, Wen wrote a full account of her sixty-eight years, including details about growing up in San Francisco, her education in China, teaching school in Guang-xi Province during the Japanese occupation, her life with her husband in Hong Kong, and her return to China to teach. She even wrote about her husband's days working for the warlord-era governments and his anti-Communist newspaper in Hong Kong. At the top of each page, she was required to write an appropriate quotation from Chairman Mao. When she was done, Wen's autobiography took up more than thirty pages. She gave it to her guard to deliver to the workers. She felt certain that the workers, now that they had her full story, would treat her better than the Red Guards.

A few days later, the same student woke her up before dawn and led her back to the interrogation room. It was snowing heavily. The same four workers sat at the table and Wen stood facing them. The older man glowered at her.

"You were married to a rich and famous man. Why did you leave him to come to China?"

Wen explained, as she had written in her autobiography, that she had received a letter from Premier Zhou Enlai, asking her to return to teach English.

"It is not so simple as that," the worker said. "You enjoyed so many material comforts and pleasures in Hong Kong. Why would you give that up to come to China, where there is none of that to enjoy?"

"I love my fatherland," Wen said. "I came to serve the people by teaching my countrymen English." She felt it was unnecessary to talk about her husband's mistresses or her desire to see her children who had moved to China after the Communist victory.

"Where is this letter from Zhou Enlai?" the worker asked.

"It was taken by the Red Guards when they came to search my house for the 'four olds,' " Wen said.

"You must write again about why you came to China," the worker said. He waved his hand to signal her to leave.

After that, the interrogation sessions continued every night. On some afternoons, Wen was taken to a different room to be interrogated by a young woman worker in a pretty silk blouse who asked her many of the same questions. Then, sometime after midnight, she was awakened to face the panel of workers. She thought of her two interrogation sessions as "day court" and "night court."

Wen refused to change her story to satisfy them. Often, in their anger, the workers would yell obscenities at her and call her a liar, a hag, and a bitch. The interrogations lasted for hours, and the workers tried to trap Wen in contradictions. She knew that her answers had to be consistent with all the self-criticisms she had written and all the hours of spoken answers.

The workers' interrogations seemed even worse to Wen than the beatings by the Red Guards. The workers were more clever and worldly than the students. They asked harder questions and asked the same questions over and over in different ways. But the interrogations and the struggle sessions, any contact with people, were still better than feeling trapped in her tiny room.

As the interrogations continued, workers and young teachers traveled to interview Shen Bixia, Wen's former housemaid, and her former students from Guangxi. The propaganda team became convinced that Wen was a Nationalist spy.

"We found out you were sent by the Nationalists to spy on our country," the older man with bushy eyebrows said. "Your school in Guangxi was run by the Nationalists. Now you must reveal your secret."

Wen simply repeated that she had come to China at Premier Zhou's request.

"That is a lie!"

"I am telling you only the truth."

"You have a sharp tongue. We will have to cut it if you do not confess. Now tell us, how did the Nationalists recruit you to be a spy?"

"I had no connection with the Nationalists. I am an English teacher."

Wen learned to hate that man. Every night, he repeated the questions for hours, sometimes adding new information—one of her neighbors had told the investigators she had heard clicking sounds from Wen's apartment, sounds that could have been from a telegraph. Her interrogator cursed her often as he tried to trip her up.

Wen lost track of time. When she was moved to the audiovisual building, she had left behind the nail she used to mark the wall. Now the days seemed to run together as a stream of interrogations, marches to the dining hall, and sleepless hours in her room.

There was still snow on the ground when the workers held a struggle session for Zhang Peicheng, a former acting president of the institute who was being held in prison. He arrived at the school auditorium in handcuffs, surrounded by four prison guards.

Zhang grew up in Shandong Province and studied in the Soviet Union as a boy in the 1930s. He married a Russian woman there and they had a son. But after 1949, Zhang divorced his wife, returned to China, and married a Chinese woman. They had six children.

At the beginning of the Cultural Revolution, Zhang was accused of being a Soviet spy and taken to the Number One Detention House. His wife committed suicide and his children were left to take care of themselves. One of them, a retarded boy, often wandered the streets of Shanghai, eating out of garbage cans.

The struggle session was mild. It seemed as if the students and teachers almost pitied Zhang. They criticized him for being a spy and for having lived in a luxurious apartment in Shanghai, but their taunts seemed half-hearted and no one struck or abused him. After the short session, the guards led Zhang to a jeep and returned him to the prison.

About two weeks later, the workers called Wen to another struggle session. They told her that she could only nod approval to their questions. Two of them led her to the platform in the third-floor reference room and put a tall hat on her head. The characters read, "A Nationalist spy." They hung a placard around her neck that read, "Nationalist spy from Hong Kong."

As she crossed the room with her head already bowed, Wen heard some teachers yelling, "Down with the spy!" On the platform, the workers tied her hands behind her back and pushed her head toward the floor. For about a half hour, they led the audience in reading Mao's quotations and singing revolutionary songs.

Then one of the workers reported on their investigation of Wen. He said she was hired by the Nationalists and sent into China with a wireless receiver and a spyglass. Then another worker began a barrage of questions.

"How did the Nationalists hire you? How much money did they give you? How many gold bars, how many houses did they build for you? Answer me!"

Wen said nothing.

The young woman from "day court" joined in.

"What secret materials did you send to your counterrevolutionary husband in Hong Kong? How often did you send him secrets?"

Wen remained silent.

Next, the older man from "night court" questioned her.

"We know you sent information with your receiver. Where is the set now? Where did you hide it? Answer me! Are you dumb?"

Each of the dozen workers in the room assaulted her with questions.

"Why were you born in America?" one man asked. "You spoke English as your spying tool—you came here behind a smoke screen as a teacher of English."

In between the questions, the members of the department joined in with shouts of "Down with Wen Zengde!" It was their last attempt to force her to confess so that she could be sentenced for her crimes.

A few weeks after the struggle session, a school worker came to visit Wen after breakfast. He unlocked the door and, as he entered the room, put his finger over his lips to signal Wen to remain silent. She recognized him—he had been working in the institute's kitchen before the propaganda team arrived.

"Quickly!" he whispered. "You must move to another room." He helped Wen gather up her clothes and straw mat and took her to a large room next door. It had two windows facing the walkway, a wooden plank for a bed, and a desk. He explained to Wen that the old team of workers had departed and a new team was coming that day. He locked the door to her new room and left.

In the days that followed, the new group of workers paid little attention to Wen. There were no struggle sessions or interrogations. In March, about a month after the new workers arrived, they moved her back to the women's dormitory. The leader of the department's propaganda team told her she had to attend political-study sessions on campus in the morning, afternoon, and evening. But she would be permitted to return to her apartment to eat lunch at noon and to sleep at night. For the first time in more than two and one-half years, Wen slept in her apartment in Friendship Village.

Wen had survived the worst days of the Cultural Revolution. She had been imprisoned and beaten for months by Red Guards, criticized and humiliated by her former colleagues and students, and isolated and interrogated by the propaganda teams. Wen's privileged background and American upbringing had made her a target. But her upbringing also had convinced her that status was not a crime and that justice would prevail. It would be another seven years before her faith was rewarded.

NINE
Baoshan
(April 1969)

In April 1969, the Ninth Party Congress met in Beijing to adopt a new constitution. The document officially recognized the importance of Mao Zedong's Thought, named Lin Biao as Mao's successor, and limited party membership to those with worker, poor farmer, and military backgrounds. The party also declared an official end to the Great Proletarian Cultural Revolution.[1] But in reality, the revolution—and the power struggles and terror that accompanied it—would continue.

During the three previous years of turmoil, China's economy had been only slightly disrupted. Its cultural and educational institutions, however, had been devastated. Jiang Qing had banned all but a few movies, ballets, and operas that she considered revolutionary, libraries and museums had been closed, and university education had been suspended. Tens of thousands of artists, writers, scientists, and scholars had been persecuted. An estimated three million cadres—as much as 20 percent of the entire bureaucracy—were purged. Many were tortured and imprisoned; most of them were sent to work in the countryside.[2]

Perhaps half a million people died from torture, murder, or suicide during the Cultural Revolution. The statistics only hint at the horror. In Guangxi Province, where Wen had escaped the Japanese in World War II, thousands of people participated in public executions, then joined in eating the flesh and organs of their victims.[3]

Between 1966 and 1969, China had isolated itself from the outside world. It prohibited most foreigners from entering the country and suspended much of its foreign commerce and diplomacy. China's relations with the Soviet Union had continued to deteriorate. In the spring of 1969, that conflict led to a series of border clashes with heavy casualties. The battles—which the Chinese apparently precipitated—provided China's leaders with an opportunity to divert the nation's attention from the excesses of the Cultural Revolution.[4] Mao sent thousands of urban youth to work at the Soviet border.

Relations with the United States also remained hostile. Fearing air raids from U.S. bombers, Mao called for a massive civil defense program in the cities. Urban residents dug tunnels and trenches to serve as air raid shelters,[5] and each household was ordered to produce a quota of unbaked bricks. Many teachers and students who remained in urban areas were sent to the countryside during the crisis.

Wen was among the first group from the institute sent to the countryside in Baoshan, a farm commune north of Shanghai, near where the Huangpu River enters the sea. (Baoshan later would become the site of a giant steel plant.) Wen and about forty other teachers and students arrived there early in April, after a dusty, bumpy two-hour trip on a long-distance bus. Several trucks brought their bunk beds from the institute. A dozen women—Wen, ten students from the English and French departments, and a young English teacher who served as Wen's guard—lived in a small room in a village dormitory. The young teacher, a fervent Maoist and party member, once had been Wen's student.

The residents of Baoshan treated the teachers with respect, despite Mao's well-known hostility to intellectuals. The peasants had survived generations of leaders and dozens of campaigns—including the disastrous famines during the Great Leap Forward in 1958–59—by adapting to or ignoring whatever their government asked of them. Some peasants saw Mao as another Buddhist icon and worshiped him in their Halls of Loyalty.

Early each morning, Wen headed out to the fields with the women farmers and other older teachers. The peasants gently taught her how to perform tasks she never had imagined doing—breaking up the soil with a hoe, pulling out weeds, and planting beans, wheat, and rice. On rainy days, Wen learned how to sort through grain and set aside those grains that would be sown into seedlings for the fall planting. The peasants appeared happy to take over Wen's work when she seemed tired.

At mealtimes, Wen lined up at the kitchen with all the other students and teachers, bowl in hand, to receive her portion of rice and watery vegetables. On some days, they would be treated to a few pieces of pork, most of it gristle. The peasants in Baoshan seemed prosperous and ate better than the teachers. At their banquets, they served plenty of pork, carp, and eel, foods that were then being rationed in Shanghai.

The kindness of the peasants surprised Wen, but she still was subject to the discipline of the propaganda teams, some of whom had accompanied the teachers and students to Baoshan. The day after she arrived, one of the workers ordered Wen to remove the nightsoil bucket from her dormitory and dump it in the communal pit.

Wen found the job difficult and humiliating; she had never imagined doing the work of a laborer. Turning her face away as she lifted the heavy bucket of feces and urine, Wen tried to hold her breath to avoid the smell. She took a few steps toward the door but didn't have the strength to carry the bucket by its handle. So she clasped it against her chest and stomach, bracing it with her arms. The contents splashed onto her clothes as she struggled out of the dormitory and down to the end of the dirt road outside the village. Then she dumped the pail into a huge pit where the nightsoil fermented to be used as fertilizer. The stench was horrible. She was assigned to repeat this task each afternoon.

Other than that, Wen rarely saw the workers from the propaganda team. They seemed to spend most of their time inside their dormitory—one of the few brick buildings in the village—drinking and playing cards. In the afternoons, when the teachers and students returned from work, the team directed them in small-group political-study sessions, chanting the familiar sayings of Chairman Mao. And there were occasional struggle sessions as well.

One afternoon a few weeks after Wen arrived, the loud-speakers on poles throughout the village broadcast an announcement that all the workers, peasants, students, and teachers were to gather in the primary school auditorium. The announcer proclaimed that this would be a meeting to "recall the past sufferings in the old society and one's happiness in the new."

Inside the auditorium, the teachers were led one by one to the podium to face accusations from the students and younger teachers. The peasants watched passively. When Wen was pushed to the stage, her former student shouted accusations at her. This old woman, she said, was a capitalist who once lived in a four-story house with fifty servants and who used to eat shark-fin soup, dove eggs, and suckling pig.

Baoshan (April 1969)

Wen tried not to smile, amused that her former student recalled some of the stories she had told in class about her life in Beijing. The young woman had exaggerated, but Wen began to remember the days at the prince's mansion and the lavish banquets with government officials. Her reverie was rudely interrupted.

"Wen Zengde, you must now eat this bitter bread," the woman commanded, "and recall the suffering of those whom you exploited. You must eat every crumb."

She held out four balls in her hand, steamed green bread made of rice husks, wild greens, and corn flour. Wen picked up one ball. It was rough and hard. She closed her eyes and tried to swallow it, but the bread scratched her throat. Wen could barely swallow the second one. But she ate all four balls without complaining; her throat was so sore that she had difficulty eating rice for the next two days.

That fall, some of the younger teachers from the institute also began to arrive in Baoshan. They helped with the fall harvest and stayed until the following summer. Unlike Wen and the older teachers, however, this group was allowed to return to Shanghai once a month to spend a weekend with their families. But not all of the young teachers would retain their privileges. Some would become victims of one of the last spasms of terror from the Cultural Revolution, accused of being "May Sixteenth elements," a secret group allegedly seeking to overthrow the government.

The May 16 plot—which may have been fictitious—was said to have begun in 1967, when a small group of radical leftists organized against Premier Zhou Enlai. As a consequence, several party leaders were purged. But the campaign against May Sixteenth plotters was revived in 1970–71. Hundreds of thousands of people were accused of having joined the secret organization. The propaganda teams in the universities conducted many of the investigations and imprisoned and tortured their suspects. Most of those who were held succumbed to pressure and confessed; some falsely accused others of belonging to the group. Many of the suicides during the Cultural Revolution occurred during this period.[6]

The propaganda teams based their accusations on information they had gathered from teachers' files and from interviews with teachers' families and associates. One of the targets at the institute was Guan Keguang, a young English teacher and another of Wen's former students. Guan was arrested in June and told to confess his crimes.

The propaganda team had learned that Guan was born in Shandong Province in 1938. His father abandoned the family when Guan was eight. Guan moved to Shanghai with his mother, where they lived with her sister and parents. After the Communist victory in 1949, Guan's father came to Shanghai and took his wife and Guan with him to Canton. But Guan's father did not stay with them long. He went to work as a clerk at a factory in Hong Kong and sent money back to Canton. After a year, Guan's father disappeared again.

Guan returned with his mother to Shanghai, where they lived with his aunts and grandparents near Yu Gardens, one of the poorest sections of the Old City. A few years later, Guan's uncle from Canton wrote him that his father had returned there and had a new wife and baby. Guan's mother divorced her husband in 1956.

But Guan's father had a secret life that he had hidden from his family. A few years after Guan had returned to Shanghai, his father was arrested, charged with being a Nationalist agent, and sentenced to seven years in prison. In 1967, unbeknownst to Guan, a Red Guard from Canton had reported the story of Guan's father to one of the teachers in the English department.

Guan had one clue about the black mark in his background. At a struggle session that year, a Red Guard stated that there was an English teacher whose father was a spy. He didn't mention Guan's name. But the information had been entered in his file, well before Guan knew the truth about his father. His family background made Guan a prime suspect in the campaign against the May Sixteenth elements.

For more than a week, the workers isolated Guan in a small hut during the day. His guards refused to let him send letters to his wife and two children and withheld all of their letters to him. Students and teachers shunned him when he walked through the village and when he returned to his bunk at night. The peasants seemed oblivious to all this. During the Dragon Boat Festival, the holiday that signals the start of summer, several of the peasants brought Guan the traditional zhongzhi dumplings, lotus leaves filled with rice and sweet red-bean paste. Guan politely refused their offerings, telling them they would get in trouble for talking with him.

In the small hut that served as his prison each day, Guan was under orders to read Mao's works and to write a confession, but he didn't know what was expected of him. The Red Guards and workers came often to give him hints and encouragement.

"Others have exposed you, your best friends. They are not defending you. Your crimes are so serious, if you do not confess, you might be executed."

Guan was afraid someone had fabricated stories against him. But he had no idea what to write, so he put down his thoughts about the party and his loyalty to Mao.

His isolation at Baoshan lasted for a week. On June 8, Guan was taken back to the institute and locked up. Only a handful of people were on the campus; the classrooms and most of the dormitories were vacant. The propaganda team isolated Guan in Room 126, a small classroom on the first floor of the English department building.

The room had a large window facing south and remained sunny throughout the day. There were five beds and several school desks and chairs. A slogan, promising leniency for those who confessed, was painted over Guan's bed. Two workers and two students were assigned to guard Guan, and at least one worker and one student remained in the room with him at all times and slept in the other beds.

Guan's guards made certain he was completely cut off from the outside world. He could leave only to use the bathroom across the hall, but they even followed him there. At mealtimes, the guards would take Guan's bowl and rice coupons and bring him back some food or soup. He had no choice in what he ate and rarely got anything besides rice and soggy vegetables. On some weekends, the guards would leave to visit their homes. They would lock Guan in the room and leave him a bucket to use as a toilet, a bowl of water, and some steamed bread.

In the first few weeks on campus, different interrogators came to question Guan and yell at him throughout the day and night. At one marathon session that lasted from 6 P.M. until well after midnight, he faced twenty different interrogators. Guan's questioners pressured him to confess, but they offered no clues as to what crimes he had committed. On some days, they left him articles from the *People's Daily* or *Red Flag* (a Communist party journal) to read.

When Guan returned to his room, his guards continued to observe him. The student guards treated him most harshly, yelling whenever they talked to him. One of his guards, Ying Daosui, was a first-year student who had never done well in his studies but had become the leader of the most radical group of Red Guards.

The workers seemed more relaxed. One was a young man nicknamed Tiger, who seemed to enjoy being a jailer and interrogator instead of working at his factory. He spent his free time catching cicadas that flew in through the window. But the other worker, the commander of this small detachment, never smiled. He was known as master worker Ding. The guards rarely spoke to Guan. Sometimes, they pulled out small brown notebooks and scribbled down their observations.

As the June rainy season came to an end, the interrogators came to visit less often. Guan spent most of his days sitting at one of the school desks, looking at a stack of writing paper and a set of Chairman Mao's works. He watched the shadow from the sunlight cross the paper and thought about what he should write.

As a boy, Guan had worried about what he had done to make his father leave him. He had become a gentle, compassionate man who was eager to please others. Now, Guan desperately wanted to satisfy his captors and confess to whatever crimes he had committed. But he didn't know what he had done wrong. He tried to guess what they expected him to write. Each day, he stared at the blank paper and sneaked glances at his guards, hoping the right words would come.

The isolation was slowly devouring him. He began to believe that all his friends had turned against him and that he was alone again. Guan felt as if he was losing control of his thoughts. He felt he was going mad.

For a few days, Guan considered suicide. It seemed to be the only way he could stop the fear and confusion. Perhaps he could climb up on a chair while his guard was asleep and stick his hand into the overhanging fluorescent light fixture. Or he could fasten his belt to the ceiling somehow and hang himself. But the thoughts of suicide didn't last long. He returned to thoughts about his family. His suicide would be an act of protest, but it would also mean his family, friends, and relatives would suffer because of their "crime of association" with Guan. His children's future would be ruined.

On July 11, a steamy Saturday night about a month after he had been imprisoned at the institute, Guan heard his four guards talking loudly outside his room. They were discussing a movie that was scheduled to be shown that night on the sports field. It was a film from Albania, the tiny, isolated Balkan country that was one of China's few remaining allies. The guards agreed they would all go together and leave Guan alone.

Before they left, one of the young workers, Tiger, entered the room. He looked at Guan, who was sitting on his bed, and walked over to another bed. Tiger reached into his back pocket and removed his notebook. Then he slid it under his pillow. He knew Guan had seen him.

The guards left for the movie and locked Guan in. For a few minutes, Guan stared at Tiger's pillow. He had to see the notebook, to find out what charges they had against him. But he feared it was a trap, a setup to catch him reading Tiger's notes.

Guan could hear the loudspeaker on the sports field from his room. The movie had started. He waited another minute, then jumped up from his bed and slipped his hand under Tiger's pillow. Guan opened the notebook and raced through the pages, afraid the guards would return at any second and surprise him.

The entries were written like a diary, a day-to-day account of Guan's imprisonment. He stopped at one page where Tiger had written some instructions. The workers had told Tiger to watch Guan carefully and prevent him from committing suicide.

Guan skipped to the front of the notebook. There were

some sketchy notes about a meeting held to discuss his case. Guan found what he was looking for—a list of charges against him. They seemed ridiculous, but Guan recognized that the crimes were serious. One charge was that he had purposely defaced a portrait of Chairman Mao. Another was that he was a member of a counterrevolutionary clique that planned to overthrow the government and make Guan prime minister. He could be executed if he was found guilty of either crime.

Guan read the charges carefully. There also was a list of minor crimes, including an allegation that he had called Jiang Qing a second-rate actress. Then Guan closed the notebook and put it back under Tiger's pillow. He was sitting on his bed when his guards returned from the movie.

For the next few weeks, Guan worked on his confession. He understood that the charges against him were based only on accusations. The guards, under Chinese law, needed his confession before they could punish him. He also suspected they had deliberately left the notebook behind. But he didn't think it was a trap. The workers simply had a quota to fill, Guan thought. Mao had said that 5 percent of the people were disloyal, and the workers had set out to confirm the wisdom of his words. Guan also believed they would be lenient with him if he confessed, but would hold him indefinitely if he didn't. He was desperate to be set free and to see his family.

In his room, Guan argued with himself until he figured out how to confess. He arrived at what he thought was a clever solution. Guan invented a story about how he had accidentally defaced a picture of Chairman Mao.

He began to write for the first time on the blank sheets of paper he had stared at for so many weeks. His story was simple. Earlier in the Cultural Revolution, Guan had been assigned to paint slogans on walls and in hallways around the campus. He also copied portraits of Chairman Mao onto the walls in department offices. The workers from the propaganda team were so impressed with Guan's work that they took him to their steel plant to paint a thirty-foot-high portait of Mao and Lin Biao on the outside of one of the factory buildings. With a ruler and pencil, Guan divided a small picture of Mao and Lin into square sections, then carefully copied each block onto the factory wall. It took Guan and a student assistant more than a week to finish.

In his confession, Guan wrote that when he finished Mao's portrait, he accidentally left a small x—a sign that a person is to be executed—on Mao's face. He asked for leniency for his error. When he finished writing, Guan took the confession to the propaganda team.

Gu, the worker who was now responsible for Guan, told Guan he was pleased with his statement. He said it was good for Guan to confess. But he wasn't completely satisfied. Gu wanted him to report other, "more serious" crimes.

In the next few days, Guan wrote about his counterrevolutionary clique. It was another artful confession, adequate to fill the workers' quota but not damaging enough to warrant serious punishment. Guan wrote that he and some other teachers had joked about setting up their own government. They had no real plans, he wrote, to overthrow the government. Nonetheless, Guan confessed, it had been an insult to Chairman Mao, and he apologized for it.

Gu read the second confession and continued to encourage Guan, telling him he was making progress. He seemed to trust Guan more now, leaving him unguarded but locked in on most days and weekends. The lectures and the interrogations stopped. Everyone seemed less stern and severe. Guan hoped he would be set free soon.

On the afternoon of September 30, the workers took Guan to the teachers' reference room on the third floor of the

English department building. The whole department was waiting there for him (Wen and the others already had returned from Baoshan), as well as the leaders of the propaganda team. It was his final criticism session.

The criticism session was a well-practiced ritual by now. It started with songs and slogans, followed by readings of quotations from Mao's works. Then, as Guan bowed his head, the teachers and students spoke out against him. They chastised Guan for being disloyal to the party and to Chairman Mao. Guan's crimes had been severe, they said. He had committed acts so terrible that they could not repeat the words or they themselves would be criminals. In addition, one of the teachers said, Guan's father had been a Nationalist spy.

Guan had been impassive, but he could not conceal his shock at this new accusation. It was the first time he had heard about the charges against his father. But he did not speak out. He was too close to freedom to lose control now. Guan listened to Gu report on his imprisonment. He said Guan had been making progress and should be given a chance to join the revolution.

Finally, Guan spoke. He admitted his crimes—although he said he had known nothing about his father's crimes—and criticized himself for failing to understand party policies. But he had studied hard, Guan said, and knew now he had been wrong. He thanked the propaganda team and the students for helping him to realize his mistakes and for generously giving him the chance to reform. Like a sinner at a revival meeting, Guan testified to the error of his ways. He was ready to rejoin the faithful.

After the meeting, Gu talked again with Guan. He encouraged him to continue studying Mao's works and warned him not to speak with his former coconspirators or to discuss his imprisonment with anyone. Gu told Guan to report to him from time to time on his progress. Guan's case was not closed. He had shown his readiness to take the first step on his road back to the side of the revolutionaries, Gu said, but there was still a long road ahead.

Guan was released after dinner. It was the day before the twenty-first anniversary of the founding of the Communist state. Gu gave Guan a final warning—he was not to commit any sabotage on National Day—then set him free. Guan had been a prisoner for 101 days. The fear would stay with him for years.

After Wen returned from Baoshan, she had registered with a propaganda team member in the English department who assigned her to a political study group. On her first day back, she walked to Friendship Village for the first time in more than a year. On her way home, she felt a sense of freedom in returning to a familiar place and routine. Wen's exhilaration was short-lived.

At her doorway, Wen found two strips of paper across the entrance, forming an X. Her apartment had been searched once again. Wen ducked under the paper and into the living room. All of the furniture had been turned over and clothes and papers were scattered on the floor.

In her bedroom, Wen found a heap of debris in front of her bed. It was a pile of torn and burned photographs, the only remaining mementos of her long, eventful life. The shreds included a photograph of her on a float in San Francisco celebrating the 1911 revolution; a 1922 picture with her new husband and their families after their wedding at the Navy Club; a photo of the palace in Beijing where they had lived; and dozens of pictures of her son and daughters. A few, including a picture of her and her brother together at a Shanghai restaurant, appeared to be missing. Wen set aside several of the torn pictures in a shoe box. Then she numbly collected the ashes in a dustpan and took them to the trash heap outside. When Wen returned to the house, she sat on her bed and cried. She had held her emotions in check for the past four years. She had learned how to lie—even to herself—about what she felt. But now the burned memories hurt too much. It was as if the Cultural Revolution, which had tried to take away her respect and pride, had stolen her past.

TEN
Shanghai
(February 1972)

 In the spring and fall of 1971, as many of the Shanghai Foreign Languages Institute's students and teachers again were sent to the countryside, Wen and her older colleagues remained in the city. She was required to work and participate in political study on campus during the day, but she stayed in her own apartment at night, free of the pressures from students, colleagues, and the propaganda team. As the months passed, however, she discovered that her home could be like a prison, too. Wen now had new, more surreptitious guards—her neighbors.

A woman Wen called Lao Hsu, the head of the neighborhood committee, lived in an apartment next door to hers. Lao Lu, a woman who taught Russian at the middle school, had the apartment on the other side. The two of them watched Wen's every move. Once, Lao Lu followed Wen to the bakery and reported that she had bought soda crackers. Wen was called before a meeting of the neighborhood committee the next evening and criticized for returning to her bourgeois, Western ways. She refused to be intimidated by her neighbors. Wen told the committee that she had broken no laws—she simply was following the law of her stomach.

On campus, political-study sessions lasted almost ten hours each day, breaking up only at mealtimes. The English department students and teachers who hadn't gone to the countryside met six days a week to read Mao's essays and quotations and to discuss them at length. Nearly every day, one of the older teachers would be ordered to stand up and list the crimes he or she had committed. Most simply stood in silence, waiting for the other teachers and students to make the now-familiar accusations.

The propaganda team also put some of the teachers to work. Wen was assigned to the brick-making squad, exempting her from most of the afternoon and evening study sessions. Her coworkers were Zhu Bingsun, the grammar teacher who had tried to kill herself; Fang Zhong, the former chairman of the English department; and some of the other older teachers who had been paraded on the sports field in 1966 and later imprisoned.

Wen's squad dug up clay, mixed it with water, and stomped on the clay with their bare feet to soften it. They then formed the clay in wooden molds and carted it to a kiln to be fired. The squad also used the bricks and mortar to build a wall around a house near the dining hall. The wall didn't appear to serve any useful purpose, and Wen found the work monotonous. Yet she was satisfied to produce something, even a meaningless wall.

On several occasions that spring and summer, Wen was called to the propaganda team office for interrogations. Four men, usually polite and friendly, sat around a square table and questioned her. On some days, they asked Wen familiar questions about her decision to come to China in 1956 and about her son, who had been labeled a rightist and remained in a labor camp. But they were rarely harsh with her and Wen was not afraid.

One day that summer, the four workers called her in to discuss her expenses. For some reason, they wanted to know how Wen had spent her salary before the Cultural Revolution began. She had been earning 150 yuan a month then—her salary was cut to 30 yuan after the revolution started—and the workers, who earned far less, told her they thought she had made a great deal of money. As Wen tried to account for her budget, an older worker interrupted her.

"I think you must have had some sweethearts to help you spend all that money," the man said. "How much did you spend on your sweethearts?"

Wen's calm demeanor quickly changed into anger. The worker not only had questioned her honesty but also was trying to intrude into her private life. She yelled back her response.

"Haven't you had enough reports from my neighbors who follow me all the time?" Wen asked. "Are you now more interested in my personal life than my political crimes? Why do you insist on bothering a seventy-year-old woman?"

Wen refused to answer any further questions that day and the workers left her alone.

Members of the English department occasionally conducted their own interrogations. One afternoon, all the English teachers assembled in the department library. Wen was told to sit opposite Chen Deyun, the young teacher with a missing eye known as the One-Eyed Dragon, who was heading the investigation. Chen came from a lower-class family and was a veteran party member. He had survived and prospered during the Cultural Revolution with his political skills—he had been among the first teachers to side secretly with the Red Guards early in the revolution, helping them find evidence against his fellow teachers and party members.

After opening the session with the required reading from Mao's quotations, Chen announced that the department was clearing class ranks, an expression suggesting that there was a spy among them. Chen pointed at Wen.

"We have found proof that you have corresponded with your husband, Chen Xiaowei, the counterrevolutionary," Chen said. "Do you have anything to say to defend yourself? We have a witness right here." Chen motioned to Fang Zhong, the former department chairman who had been Wen's friend for years.

Fang looked away nervously and thumbed through a notebook.

"May I say a few words?" Wen asked. Chen nodded.

Wen stared coldly at Fang. "How did you know I wrote my husband?" she asked. "Did you see me mail him a letter?"

"You once told me that you had sent him a letter through his mistress," Fang replied.

"When did I tell you this? Where were we when we talked? What more did I tell you?"

Fang hesitated.

"Please, tell me the time, the place, and the date. Otherwise, you will be making a fool of yourself."

Fang did not answer. But Chen said they had other evidence of her disloyalty. When they searched her apartment, he said, they had found a photograph of her and her husband together. Chen handed it to Wen.

Wen laughed. The man in the photo, she said, was not her husband but her brother, Wen Xingfei. It had been taken at a farewell dinner in the 1930s, just before he left his teaching post at Fudan University in Shanghai and moved to Guangxi Province.

"You're a liar," the One-Eyed Dragon yelled. "You have the mouth of a pig."

Wen remained calm. She invited her accusers to take the

photograph to Fudan and ask the older teachers there to identify the man in the picture. Or, she said, they could visit a Shanghai hotel, where her brother's son was staying. If either the professors or her nephew identified the man as Chen Xiaowei, Wen said, she would willingly accept a sentence of life imprisonment. Her forceful response put an end to the investigation, and nothing more ever came of the charges.

But Wen did discover why Fang had betrayed her. She learned later that the propaganda team had offered to pay him his back salary—nearly eight thousand yuan, the amount his salary had been reduced over the past five years—if he would make accusations against her.

Wen never talked with Fang after that. When he approached, she simply bowed her head and walked on. It saddened her to know that the Cultural Revolution had turned friends and family members against each other and made victims into victimizers. What seemed worse, however, was that truth and trust were no longer valued. Those who could lie and scheme not only survived, but profited.

While Wen and her colleagues worked and studied on campus, two groups of younger teachers had been sent to a small village in Anhui Province. They were assigned to what was known as a May Seventh Cadre School. Mao had created the schools in a directive on May 7, 1966, when he called on party officials to go to the countryside and learn from the peasants. The first school was opened in Heilongjiang Province, the most remote province in northeastern China. Eventually, as many as three million cadres were sent to hundreds of different schools in remote areas of the country.[1]

The cadre school for the Foreign Languages Institute was in a village called Fengyang, more than 250 miles north of

Shanghai. It had been the birthplace of the first Ming emperor more than six centuries earlier but now was a poor, dusty village where crippled beggars crawled on the streets. The only reminders of its noble past—it had been the emperor's capital for a short time—were the tomb of the emperor's parents and two long rows of statues portraying horses, rams, lions, unicorns, and nine-foot-tall generals. Early in the Cultural Revolution, Red Guards had beheaded and smashed nearly all of the ancient statues.

In Fengyang, the institute's teachers and cadres dug ponds, built dams, fertilized crops, and planted trees and vegetables. Some of them lived temporarily in huts with the village peasants. The teachers worked hard and had only two days off each month, every other Sunday when they could go to a farmers' market. That summer and fall, the young teachers, most of whom looked tanned and healthy, started to come back to Shanghai. The Foreign Languages Institute was about to reopen as a university.

In the fall of 1971, the institute enrolled new students for the first time in five years. The national entrance examinations had been abolished, and college students now were selected on the basis of recommendations and political background, increasing the numbers of working-class pupils. All prospective students were required to work as manual laborers before they could attend college. The form and content of higher education were transformed as well.[2]

Undergraduates would attend college for about three years, instead of the previous four- or five-year system. Government policy called for a shorter school year and simpler courses, with an emphasis on practical training. The schools also were expected to use simplified teaching materials, based on Mao's Thought. But each school would develop its own curriculum and teaching materials.[3]

In the institute's English department, the first texts were

simply English translations of Mao's Thought. One was a
ten-page pamphlet of quotations and phrases. "We must
study Chairman Mao's works every day," one translation
read. "If we miss one day, problems will pile up. Let two
days pass, and we start slipping backwards. Three days
makes it impossible to live." Another read: "The heavens are
great, the earth is great, but they can't compare with the
greatness of what the Party has done for the people. Dear as
are father and mother, Chairman Mao is still dearer."[4]

Even the most fervent Maoists on the faculty soon realized
that such texts were inadequate for a university education.
So the department assigned a group of teachers to write new
conversation materials. Wen's native English skills once again
became valued in the English department.

She worked under the supervision of five English teachers,
two from the Foreign Languages Institute and three from the
Foreign Trade Institute. Several other teachers worked with
Wen, including Guan Keguang and Hou Weirui. Hou, the
radical young teacher who had led the campaigns against the
older faculty, was no longer in a position of power. During
the May Sixteenth campaign, Hou, like Guan, was among
those who were imprisoned.

The teachers' first job was to rewrite and simplify foreign
articles for conversation classes. In the first few months, they
could use material only from leftist and Communist foreign
papers, such as *People's Voice* in New Zealand and *Vanguard*
in Australia. For a time, the American radical paper, the
Guardian, was an acceptable source, but it was later dropped
when the paper criticized the Chinese Communist party. The
articles had to be both practical and politically acceptable.

One article they considered came from *People's Voice.* It
was written by a New Zealand journalist about his visit to
Rome with his son. According to this account, the boy found
that there were many poor people in capitalist societies and

that citizens were beaten by police. But in China, the boy said, there was no crime and the people were much more friendly. The group readily approved the article.

Members of the propaganda team had final review over the teachers' selections. But none of the team members could read English, so the teachers translated the English articles into Chinese for them. After the propaganda team approved an article, the group had it typed and reproduced at the school print shop. Wen and the other teachers had to be particularly careful when they proofread the printed articles.

The difficulty wasn't typographical errors but political ones. Revered names, like Mao Zedong, could not appear near inflammatory words, like "running dogs," or near negative words, like "death" or "bad." The prohibition applied even to the reverse side of the thin pages. The teachers had to hold all the pages up to the light to make sure China's leaders weren't being inadvertently slandered by a word that showed through.

Wen also was given the task of writing dialogues. Her supervisors assigned ideas to her; they still didn't trust her to work completely on her own. Her first assignment was to write a dialogue titled "A Foreigner Seeing a Doctor of Traditional Chinese Medicine."

Wen took on the job with her usual vigor and thoroughness. She had little formal background in Chinese medicine, so she began by doing some research. She first approached an older teacher who had collected books on traditional medicine. The teacher was polite, but told Wen he could not help because of the accusations that had been made against her. Then she tried the school library.

In China's universities, libraries often function like vaults—even in the best of times—restricting rather than widening access to books and periodicals. Most college libraries were closed during the Cultural Revolution and many materials had been banned. Once colleges reopened, faculty members could use the libraries only with special permission, and there were strict controls on who could take out books. The Foreign Languages Institute's librarian turned Wen away. She was still considered unfit to browse through the handful of books, magazines, and newspapers the library now held.

Undaunted, Wen pursued her research in the spirit of the new educational reforms. She would rely on the practical, not the theoretical. Wen took a bus to Longhua Hospital in the southern part of the city to visit some Chinese doctors she knew.

The doctors were eager to help and provided her with dozens of Chinese and English articles from their affiliated medical academy, covering everything from colds to stomach ailments. They also taught her the principles of Chinese medicine and how to examine a patient by asking about symptoms, checking the pulse and skin complexion, and smelling the patient's breath. Wen was excited by her new knowledge and, with the doctors' help, wrote a dialogue about a foreigner with a recurrent fever who was leaving China and had asked a Chinese doctor for medicinal herbs to take with him.

Wen did similar research for other dialogues. She talked with a physical education instructor for the conversations she was assigned to write on table tennis and calisthenics. Arthur Mayer, a Portuguese national who had been teaching at the institute for more than a decade, helped her write a dialogue, "A Toast of Farewell to a Foreign Friend," about a foreign visitor leaving China.

Some of the stories and dialogues caused trouble, even after they had been approved by the supervisors and the propaganda team and carefully proofread. For one of the reading classes, the English teachers had translated an ancient fable, "Six Blind Men and the Elephant." The tale concerns six blind Indian beggars who come upon an elephant and feel different parts of its body, trying to guess what they are touching. The teachers attempted to avoid possible political pitfalls in their translation. They rewrote the story so that it didn't mention India, another of China's neighbors embroiled in a long-standing border dispute. They also decided that the men in the story should not be beggars, because beggars were considered proletarian. It would be unwise, they thought, to write a humorous tale that poked fun at poor people. In the final version of the revised story, the Indian beggars became classless people with no nationality. But the moral of the story remained the same: It is dangerous to draw conclusions with only part of the truth.

The supervisors and propaganda team members approved the text and the teachers had it printed. The copies were distributed to the classroom teachers, who gave them to their students a few weeks later. But the new working-class students found a message in the fable that the teachers hadn't anticipated.

When Wen and the other teachers in the group reported to work that week, they found the hallways of the English department covered with wall posters, just as they had been at the start of the Cultural Revolution five years earlier. The posters denounced the teachers and criticized the tale as an insult to working people. To the new students, the story suggested that common people were stupid and couldn't see what was in front of them. That, they felt, was the view of elitist intellectuals.

Later that week, the teachers in the group attended one of the English classes to meet with the students. For nearly two hours, the students angrily criticized them for making fun of the poor and the workers. They said that the teachers needed to be reeducated. Wen and her colleagues then stood before the students, made self-criticisms, and apologized. At a schoolwide meeting a few days later, the head of the propaganda team pointed out the English students who had criticized the teachers and praised them for their vigilance.

As university education was being transformed in the fall of 1971, extraordinary changes were taking place in Beijing. The nation's second-highest-ranking official, Lin Biao, had fallen from power and died. Lin, who had been Mao's designated successor, was accused of plotting against him and reportedly had been killed in a plane crash in Mongolia.

Historians can now only speculate on the reasons for Lin's fall and the circumstances of his death. Lin apparently angered Mao after the Ninth Party Congress in 1969 when he urged Mao to resume his position as head of state. Mao wanted the mostly ceremonial post abolished, but Lin persisted, leading to speculation that he wanted the position for himself if Mao should turn it down. Mao rallied his supporters to defeat Lin's proposal.[5]

In the meantime, Chinese relations with the Soviet Union had become increasingly hostile as border clashes continued. China's allies in Eastern Europe passed on rumors that the Soviets planned to attack Chinese nuclear installations. Despite Lin's apparent opposition, Chinese leaders secretly began to explore possible ties with the United States.[6]

According to evidence later presented at the trial of Lin's supporters, he and his family began plotting a coup in February 1971. It included plans to assassinate Mao. But the plot failed that fall, and Lin and his family escaped. It remains unclear whether Lin planned to set up a rival regime in Canton or to fly to the Soviet Union for sanctuary. The government reported he and his family had died in a plane crash in Mongolia—on their way to the Soviet Union—after midnight on September 13.[7]

The opening to the United States that followed was an even more remarkable reversal. Antagonism to the United States had been a driving force in Chinese foreign policy for decades. The wars in Korea and Vietnam had solidified the Chinese view that Americans were imperialist aggressors committed to the defeat of Communism. China's growing distrust of the Soviets in the late 1950s was exacerbated by Khrushchev's talks on peaceful coexistence with President Eisenhower at Camp David in 1959. And the Cultural Revolution itself had been inspired by Mao's fear that the Chinese would embrace the same revisionist policies as the Soviets.[8]

This incredible shift in Chinese policy was again largely the work of Mao. He hoped to restore China's position in the world and to establish it as a major power. The policy also was driven by the continuing Soviet threat, the beginning of U.S. withdrawal from Vietnam, and the Nixon administration's slow but positive response to China's overtures. By the spring of 1971, China and the United States were regularly engaged in secret contacts.[9]

The dalliance became public in April 1971, when a Chinese table-tennis team playing in Japan officially invited fifteen U.S. players to China. The players were accompanied by U.S. reporters and their visit generated worldwide publicity. A short time later, Edgar Snow reported that Mao had told him Nixon would be welcome in China "either as a tourist or as President." In July, Nixon's national security assistant, Henry Kissinger, on a diplomatic mission to Asia, secretly flew to Beijing to meet with Premier Zhou Enlai. Kissinger returned to Beijing in the fall to help make preparations for Nixon's visit.[10]

On February 21, 1972, Nixon, along with a party of seven hundred aides and reporters, arrived in Beijing. The U.S. delegation seemed overwhelmed by Chinese hospitality—at a welcoming banquet in Beijing, a Chinese military orchestra played "Turkey in the Straw." Nixon met with Mao on his first evening in China, and the *People's Daily* the next day displayed a front-page photograph of the two leaders shaking hands. The president also visited the Great Wall and toured Beijing, Hangzhou, and Shanghai,[11] where he was to sign a diplomatic accord.

The day before Nixon came to Shanghai, Wen Zengde was preparing conversation materials in the English department when her supervisor, Chen Deyun (The "One-Eyed Dragon"), told her to stop work and took her to a classroom near the school auditorium.

"Nixon is coming," Chen told her. "You rest here for a while." Then he locked Wen inside the classroom, the same way she had been imprisoned by the Red Guards and workers for two and one-half years. Chen apparently considered Wen a security risk. Thousands of others were detained that week, purportedly to prevent a disturbance. All along Nixon's route through the city, police searched houses and apartments and stood guard by windows as the entourage passed. Wen wasn't released from her confinement until the day after Nixon had left the country.

On February 28, at a club across from the Jin Jiang Hotel, the two nations signed a communiqué calling for further contacts and progress toward normal relations. The United States also accepted China's position that Taiwan was part of China and pledged to withdraw U.S. forces from the island.[12] It was a major diplomatic victory for China.

After Nixon's visit, Chen assigned Wen to a new job. Instead of preparing course materials, she was to clean up around campus and sweep the corridors and stairs of the English department building. Chen gave her a broom, a long-handled dustpan, and a piece of old cloth. Each day after that, Wen came to work wearing a cloth dusting cap and a knee-length apron.

Chen made sure that Wen was cleaning when the students and teachers were going to and from their classes, hoping to humiliate her. At first, Wen turned away when she saw people approaching. The indignity of working as a laborer in front of her students and colleagues was difficult for her to accept.

Wen had come from a privileged background. She had been served by maids and amahs in her days in Beijing and Hong Kong; she even had a housemaid to cook meals for her in Shanghai before the Cultural Revolution. In Wen's world, it was the workers, not intellectuals and the wealthy, who performed physical labor. The stares and whispers of the passing students and teachers wounded her; she felt ashamed. She was no longer a respected teacher but merely an old cleaning lady, bending over slowly to pick up trash and shuffling through the halls with a broom.

But Wen's fierce pride—which she had sustained throughout the years of imprisonment, interrogations, and criticism sessions, the scorn of her neighbors, and the labor in the countryside—won out. She convinced herself that Chen, who, like most of the young teachers, had once been her student, was himself the one facing humiliation. It was he who had lost face by making her do this work, she told herself. Wen decided to treat her job as a joke, to laugh at her predicament. At the end of two weeks, Chen told her to resume her work on the conversation materials.

The Sino-American rapprochement developed slowly in the following years as the final drama of the Cultural Revolution played itself out. Zhou Enlai and his followers hoped to return some stability to China and put an end to the years of turmoil. Zhou also advocated returning to the educational system that favored intellectuals, and he supported funding for scientific research.[13] Mao's wife, Jiang Qing, and her radical leftist allies called for continued revolution and struggle. They also strongly backed the educational policies that provided working-class students access to higher education.[14]

In the summer of 1973, the provinces of China conducted unified college entrance examinations in an effort to restore the system that had been abandoned in 1966.[15] The radical leftists objected, making their case through the story of Zhang Tiesheng. Zhang was a young student who had been sent to the countryside and refused to take the entrance examination, complaining it was unfair. He handed in a blank exam and wrote a letter to the examiners, saying his work had left him no time to study. Mao's nephew, an ally of the radicals, published Zhang's story as an example of discrimination against the working class. It set off a campaign to discontinue the exams, with the media featuring articles about students like Zhang who had rebelled against their teachers.[16] (After the radicals were overthrown, Zhang was exposed as a fake who had tried to pass the exam but could answer only a handful of questions. In 1983, Zhang's fortunes came full circle: he was tried as a counterrevolutionary and sent to prison.)[17]

That fall, the radicals broadened their attacks and attempted to undermine Zhou Enlai, who was terminally ill with cancer. Jiang Qing also orchestrated a campaign to set herself up as Mao's successor. In 1974, with Mao away from Beijing for most of the year, she greeted foreign leaders, appeared on television regularly, and was praised and pictured in newspapers nearly every day. The press, which was controlled by the radicals, also elevated her status with a series of articles rehabilitating two previously despised Chinese empresses. Jiang hoped to promote the idea of a female ruler of China.[18] At a politburo meeting that summer, Mao criticized his wife and called her and her three radical allies a "Gang of Four."[19]

In February 1974, the institute announced that the verdicts issued against many of the teachers and cadres during the Cultural Revolution had been reversed. Their cases had been restudied, party officials told them, and the party had concluded that many people had been dealt with too severely. Their decision was inspired by a party directive ordering work units to "give those who could be helped a hand to pull them over to the side of the people." But Wen had not confessed and a verdict had never been issued. She could not be pardoned, and she still faced the stigma of the accusations that had been made against her.

That spring, the English department's party secretary, Jin Xinzhu, called Wen to his office on another matter. Wen was about to turn seventy-four, Jin noted, and the department felt it was time for her to consider retirement. But Wen told him she wanted to continue teaching and make up for the years she had lost during the Cultural Revolution. The secretary agreed to consider her request.

The department officials decided instead to pressure Wen into retirement. They apparently were afraid she would never agree to leave. Two years earlier, the department had faced a similar problem when another foreign-born teacher had retired.

Arthur Mayer, a Portuguese national, had been a valued member of the English department who somehow had survived the Cultural Revolution without drawing much attention. But in June 1972, the school suddenly ordered Mayer to retire. Without explanation, the administration gave him only thirty-six hours to leave Shanghai. Mayer, a garrulous and sometimes boastful elderly man, wouldn't leave so easily. He asked the school to explain why he was being forced to leave and threatened to stay in Shanghai until he received an answer. The officials placated Mayer with a farewell parade, sending him home in a limousine decorated with red banners that was followed by a truck full of students beating drums and gongs. The English department sponsored a party at Mayer's home near Suzhou Creek.

That incident had deeply embarrassed the school officials, and they had no patience for another reluctant retiree. The day after Wen had been asked to retire, she found a crowd gathered by the bulletin boards outside the English department building, the same place where Wen had seen the poster for the Monster-beating Assembly eight years earlier. Now the posters concerned Wen's retirement.

The posters were neatly arranged inside the glass cases. A few offered kind words about Wen's teaching, but dozens more attacked her for teaching students a bourgeois lifestyle. Wen looked at only a few of the posters. The words made her feel sad instead of angry or humiliated. After so many years of criticism, she felt immune to the familiar insults. But she wasn't prepared for another fight. Wen decided it was time for her to retire from the institute, and she told the secretary of her decision.

A few days later, the department sponsored a farewell party for Wen. It was a low-key affair, with only candy, tea, and soda. One by one, teachers and officials stood up to speak. Fang Zhong, the department chairman who had betrayed Wen to earn his back pay, thanked her for her hard work. The department secretary, who helped the students write wall posters against Wen, praised her efforts to find material for the conversation exercises and said young teachers could learn much from her. Even Chen Deyun, who had imprisoned her during Nixon's visit and tried to humiliate her by assigning her to sweep the floors, spoke of Wen's contributions. The lies of praise seemed to flow as easily as the lies of condemnation that she had heard so many times before.

Wen accepted the thanks of her colleagues and told them she had done the best she could. "Perhaps my teaching and writing has not been as good as that of the rest of you," Wen said. "But you are Chinese and I am only a foreigner."

That night, Wen returned home to write a letter to her husband, the first time she had written him in nearly eight years. She told him the school had accepted her resignation and she was now free to travel. Perhaps, she wrote, she would come visit him in Hong Kong sometime. She wished him good health. A few weeks later, her niece's husband brought word that Chen had died just a few days before Wen's letter arrived.

By the beginning of 1975, the conservative leadership in Beijing seemed firmly in control. The National People's Congress had endorsed Zhou Enlai's "four modernizations," his proposals to stabilize the country and modernize agriculture, industry, science and technology, and defense. Deng Xiaoping, who had been ousted along with Liu Shaoqi at the beginning of the Cultural Revolution, had returned to power. Deng was named first vice premier, displacing a young member of the Gang of Four and becoming third in the line of succession behind Mao and Zhou. The Gang still controlled the media, education, and culture, but they had few positions in the official power structure.[20]

The Gang of Four's next campaign began that summer. At first, they attacked Zhou, Deng, and their followers by reinterpreting the *Water Margin,* an ancient Chinese fable about a twelfth-century peasant uprising against corrupt officials. Their allegorical attack suggested Zhou and Deng were traitors. That fall, the Gang became more direct, openly criticizing Deng's educational policies. They used their control of newspapers and television to argue that his attempt to import Western scientific training and technology would not help China but only weaken Chinese culture and political will.[21] Near the end of the year, Mao, who seemingly had been ambivalent in his support for Deng, prepared to withdraw his backing.[22]

On January 8, 1976, Deng's mentor, Zhou Enlai, died in the hospital where he had been treated for cancer for nearly two years. Zhou had become China's most revered and loved leader. Through all the years of turmoil, he was seen as the one stabilizing, humane force in the country's leadership. But members of the Gang of Four, spurned by Mao in their bid to succeed Zhou, tried to limit official mourning and public recognition for the late premier.[23]

The anger against the Gang grew in the weeks after Zhou's death and reached full force in March and April, when thousands of people brought wreaths to Tiananmen Square to honor Zhou during the annual festival to pay homage to dead relatives. On the day of the festival, April 4, as many as two million people visited the square to place wreaths and read tributes to Zhou. Many of the eulogies also criticized the Gang of Four. Before dawn the next morning, police cleared the square of wreaths and arrested those from the crowd who had remained there. Within hours, thousands of people had gathered. Protesters brought demands to the leaders, who watched the demonstrations from the Great Hall of the People. Angry students overturned and burned cars and trucks and stormed and set fire to the Public Security Bureau barracks near the square. By late in the evening, most of the crowd had responded to appeals to disperse. But the hundreds who remained were stunned by an attack from soldiers and police, who beat the demonstrators with sticks and arrested many of them. The party leadership placed the blame for the unrest on Deng Xiaoping and ousted him from power. The Gang then organized a massive rally in Tiananmen of workers, students, and soldiers in support of Mao and their policies.[24]

But the forces of nature brought portents of upheaval. On July 28, a massive earthquake destroyed Tangshan, a city only one hundred miles east of Beijing, killing 242,000 people. Residents of the capital moved into the streets, fearing an aftershock. On September 5, Mao Zedong, who suffered from Parkinson's disease, lapsed into unconsciousness. He died four days later, aged eighty-three. Without Mao's support, Jiang Qing and her associates in the Gang of Four could not hold on to their power. On October 6–7, they were arrested and held for trial. The Cultural Revolution had ended.[25]

In Shanghai, students celebrated the fall of the Gang of Four by painting slogans in the streets. The police stood by and watched. Officials at the Shanghai Foreign Languages Institute called a meeting in the school auditorium at 10 A.M. the next day to officially announce the arrest of the Gang. Some teachers joined in a parade down Nanjing Road that afternoon as students beat drums and repeatedly chanted "Down with the Gang of Four." The festive mood continued through the night. It was crab season in China, and many people celebrated by buying four crabs—three males and one female, the same as the Gang of Four—and eating them with rice wine.

Within a few weeks, the workers from the propaganda team had left the institute and returned to their factories. Over the next year, each of the school's teachers who had been accused of crimes was rehabilitated. The denunciations had come in front of the whole school; the rehabilitations came with little fanfare.

Since her forced retirement, Wen had been teaching English

part-time at local hospitals, factories, and colleges. In May 1977 the English department invited her to a meeting, where Jin Xinzhu, the party secretary, announced that Wen, too, had been wronged. "The school appreciates that Wen Zengde gave up her job in Hong Kong and came back to China to teach," Jin said. "It was wrong to call her bourgeois during the Cultural Revolution—she had left America to come back to China."

After the meeting, Jin took Wen to his office, where he showed her a stack of the self-criticisms she had written for the Red Guards and the propaganda teams. The department had saved them, but Jin now offered to burn them for her.

"Look at this big heap," he said. "What a waste of paper!" Wen laughed.

"No, it wasn't a waste," she replied, with only a slight twinge of irony. "This was my reeducation."

Epilogue

In 1979, Wen made plans to visit her two older sisters, who were still living in California. But she would not leave China until she was assured that her son, Daniel, would be released from labor camp. He had been rehabilitated that year but remained imprisoned. Wen dug her old U.S. passport out of the flowerpot on her balcony—where she had buried it thirteen years earlier—and went to the U.S. embassy in Beijing to argue her son's case. A few months later, Daniel was released; he left for the United States in 1980. Wen joined him two years later.

After Wen finally had returned to her childhood home, she decided to stay in the United States. She never saw China again. Wen spent the rest of her life in a housing project for the elderly in a rundown Oakland neighborhood, not far from the part of Chinatown in San Francisco where she had grown up more than seven decades earlier. But she still had a remarkable story to tell.

I first met Wen in Oakland in the summer of 1987, and I continued to correspond with her and ask questions about her life. Wen worked on her answers with the same vigor with which she had approached her teaching. But her letters stopped coming late in the winter of 1988. That spring, Wen sent me a brief note, explaining apologetically that she had fallen from a chair while reaching into her closet. Daniel later told me she actually had suffered a stroke and was partially paralyzed.

I arranged to visit that summer. Although I had more questions to ask, I feared for her health. A few weeks before my scheduled arrival, Wen suffered another stroke. But she wrote that she was improving quickly and insisted that I come to Oakland.

When I arrived in August, Wen seemed weaker than the previous year but in great spirits. We met in her apartment again and she dismissed my concerns about her health. (Daniel had been giving her ginseng root to chew on to give her strength.) She encouraged me to ask her more questions, but said she was worried that her memory seemed to be failing her. Perhaps, she said, I had wasted a trip. My questions seemed to fortify her. For nearly a week, we talked from the early morning into the evening. One morning, when I slept late in my motel room, Wen telephoned me at 7:30 to ask why I was delayed. There was only one change from our routine the previous summer. Instead of going out for lunches in Chinatown, she had Daniel bring us takeout. I knew she was trying to conserve her strength, but Wen told me we would save time by eating in her apartment.

When we hugged at the end of the week and said goodbye, I think both of us sensed it would be the last time we would see each other. The day after I left, Wen was admitted to an Oakland hospital. She died three days later.

Notes

Most of the material in this book is drawn from a series of interviews with Wen Zengde, Daniel Chen, and Guan Keguang, as well as with several others who have asked not to be identified, including teachers and students from the Shanghai Foreign Languages Institute and Wen's relatives. Some material, including descriptions of Shanghai, the Foreign Languages Institute, and Fengyang, is based on firsthand observation.

Prologue (November 1966)

1. Anne F. Thurston, *Enemies of the People* (New York: Alfred A. Knopf, 1987), 115.

ONE: San Francisco (1910)

1. John K. Fairbank, *The United States and China,* 4th ed. (Cambridge, Mass.: Harvard University Press, 1983), 207.
2. Congress, House, Committee on Immigration, *Importing Women for Immoral Purposes,* 61st Cong., 1909, Document 196.
3. Doris Muscatine, *Old San Francisco* (New York: G. P. Putnam's Sons, 1975), 205.

4. Ibid., 396.

5. Ibid., 388; and William Issel and Robert W. Cherny, *San Francisco, 1865–1932* (Berkeley and Los Angeles: University of California Press, 1986), 70–73.

6. Muscatine, *Old San Francisco*, 389–90, 397.

7. Ibid., 390, 403.

8. Ibid., 391.

9. Issel and Cherny, *San Francisco, 1865–1932*, 70–71.

10. Ibid.

11. Frank G. Carpenter, *China* (Garden City, N.Y.: Doubleday, Page, 1926), 57–58.

12. C. E. Darwent, *Shanghai: A Handbook for Travellers and Residents*, 2nd ed. (Shanghai: Kelly and Walsh, 1920), 6–10.

13. Ibid., 13.

TWO: Beijing (1919)

1. Philip West, *Yenching University and Sino-Western Relations, 1916–1952* (Cambridge, Mass.: Harvard University Press, 1976), 34–35, 91.

2. Vera Schwarcz, *The Chinese Enlightenment* (Berkeley and Los Angeles: University of California Press, 1986), 14–15.

3. John K. Fairbank, ed., *Republican China, 1912–1949, Part 1,* The Cambridge History of China, vol. 12 (New York: Cambridge University Press, 1983), 407.

4. Schwarcz, *The Chinese Enlightenment*, 244–50.

5. John K. Fairbank and Albert Feuerwerker, eds., *Republican China, 1912–1949, Part 2,* The Cambridge History of China, vol. 13 (New York: Cambridge University Press, 1986), 367.

6. Ibid., 363.

7. Ibid., 368–69.

8. Ibid., 377.

9. Ibid., 372.

10. Ibid., 364–65.

11. Lucian W. Pye, *Warlord Politics: Conflict and Coalition in the Modernization of Republican China* (New York: Praeger 1971), 3–9; and Andrew J. Nathan, *Peking Politics, 1918–23:*

Factionalism and the Failure of Constitutionalism (Berkeley and Los Angeles: University of California Press, 1976), 71.

12. Howard L. Boorman and Richard Howard, *Biographical Dictionary of Republican China* (New York: Columbia University Press, 1967–71), 3:376–78.

13. Ibid., 1:382–84.

14. Nathan, *Peking Politics*, 68.

15. Ibid., 83–84; and Fairbank, *Republican China, Part 1*, 268–69.

16. Sidney D. Gamble, *Peking: A Social Survey* (New York: George H. Doran, 1921), 242–63.

17. John K. Fairbank, *The Great Chinese Revolution: 1800–1985* (New York: Harper & Row, 1986), 212.

18. Ibid., 214–15.

19. Ibid., 215.

20. *All about Shanghai and Environs* (Shanghai: University Press, 1935), 45.

21. Fairbank, *The Great Chinese Revolution*, 217–25.

22. Ibid., 225–32.

23. Fairbank and Feuerwerker, *Republican China, Part 2*, 548.

24. Ibid., 552.

THREE: Hong Kong (1936)

1. G. B. Endacott, *A History of Hong Kong* (London: Oxford University Press, 1958), 289.

2. Kan Lai-bing and Grace H. L. Chu, *Newspapers of Hong Kong: 1841–1979* (Hong Kong: University Library System, Chinese University of Hong Kong, 1981).

3. Ibid.

4. Ted Ferguson, *Desperate Siege: The Battle of Hong Kong* (New York: Doubleday, 1980).

FOUR: Guangxi Province (1942)

1. Phil Billingsley, *Bandits in Republican China* (Stanford, Calif.: Stanford University Press, 1988), 38.

2. Ibid., 18–19.

3. Ibid., 166–73.

4. Ibid., 147.

5. Wolfram Eberhard, *China's Minorities: Yesterday and Today* (Belmont, Calif.: Wadsworth, 1982), 82.

6. Ibid., 84.

7. Ibid., 3–4.

8. Ibid., 125–26.

9. Ibid., 83.

10. Ibid., 146.

11. Ibid., 84.

12. Fairbank and Feuerwerker, *Republican China, Part 2*, 580–83.

FIVE: Hong Kong (1955)

1. Dick Wilson, *Zhou Enlai* (New York: Viking Press, 1984), 206–7.

2. Boorman and Howard, *Biographical Dictionary*, I: 105–9.

3. Fairbank, *The Great Chinese Revolution*, 277–81.

4. Roderick MacFarquhar and John K. Fairbank, eds., *The People's Republic of China, Part 1: The Emergence of Revolutionary China, 1949–1962*, The Cambridge History of China, vol. 14 (New York: Cambridge University Press, 1987), 193–96.

5. Ibid., 197–200.

6. Ibid., 200, 208.

7. Fairbank, *The Great Chinese Revolution*, 292; Thurston, *Enemies of the People*, 62–65.

8. Thurston, *Enemies of the People*, 62–65.

9. Ibid., 63–65.

10. MacFarquhar and Fairbank, *The Emergence of Revolutionary China*, 216.

11. Thurston, *Enemies of the People*, 62–65; Franz Schurmann and Orville Schell, eds., *Communist China, The China Reader*, vol. 3 (New York: Vintage Books, 1967), 150–55.

12. Fairbank, *The Great Chinese Revolution*, 293.

13. Schurmann and Schell, *Communist China*, 154–55.

14. Jonathan D. Spence, *The Search for Modern China* (New York: W. W. Norton, 1990), 572.

15. Ibid.

16. William A. Joseph, Christine P. W. Wong, and David Zweig, eds., *New Perspectives on the Cultural Revolution* (Cambridge, Mass.: Council on East Asian Studies/Harvard University, 1991), 84, 88.

17. Roderick MacFarquhar and John K. Fairbank, eds., *The People's Republic of China, Part 2: Revolutions Within the Chinese Revolution, 1966–1982*, vol. 15 (New York: Cambridge University Press, 1991), 560–61.

18. Neale Hunter, *Shanghai Journal* (New York: Oxford University Press, 1988), 43–44.

SIX: Shanghai (August 1966)

1. MacFarquhar and Fairbank, *Revolutions Within the Chinese Revolution,* 107.

2. Ibid., 322.

3. Ibid., 81.

4. Ibid., 110, 113, and 202.

5. Ibid., 121.

6. Ibid., 134–35.

7. Ibid., 135.

8. Ibid., 135–37.

9. Fairbank, *The Great Chinese Revolution,* 327; and Robert Jay Lifton, *Revolutionary Immortality: Mao Tse-tung and the Chinese Cultural Revolution* (New York: Vintage Books, 1968), 92–93.

10. MacFarquhar and Fairbank, *Revolutions Within the Chinese Revolution,* 138–39.

11. Fairbank, *The Great Chinese Revolution,* 327–28; and David Milton, Nancy Milton, and Franz Schurmann, eds., *People's China, The China Reader,* vol. 4 (New York: Vintage Books, 1974), 272–83.

12. Joseph, Wong, and Zweig, *New Perspectives,* 97.

13. Susan L. Shirk, *Competitive Comrades* (Berkeley and Los Angeles: University of California Press, 1982), 8–15.

14. Thurston, *Enemies of the People,* 138.

15. *Quotations from Chairman Mao Tsetung* (Beijing: Foreign Languages Press, 1972), 11–12.

SEVEN: Shanghai (November 1966)

1. MacFarquhar and Fairbank, *Revolutions Within the Chinese Revolution,* 143.

2. Fairbank, *The Great Chinese Revolution,* 328.

3. Thurston, *Enemies of the People,* 96–99.

4. Ibid., 99–105.

5. Ibid.

6. Ibid.

7. MacFarquhar and Fairbank, *Revolutions Within the Chinese Revolution,* 144–47, 150.

8. Robert van Gulik, trans., *Celebrated Cases of Judge Dee* (Tokyo, 1949; New York: Dover, 1976), xviii–xix.

9. Ibid.

10. Robert Jay Lifton, "Chinese Communist 'Thought Reform': Confession and Re-education of Western Civilians," *Bulletin, New York Academy of Medicine* 33, no. 9 (September 1957): 626–44.

11. Ibid.

12. Ibid.

EIGHT: Shanghai (August 1968)

1. MacFarquhar and Fairbank, *Revolutions Within the Chinese Revolution,* 153, 158–60.

2. Fairbank, *The Great Chinese Revolution,* 330.

3. MacFarquhar and Fairbank, *Revolutions Within the Chinese Revolution,* 179–82.

4. Ibid., 187–88.

5. Thurston, *Enemies of the People,* 121–22.

6. MacFarquhar and Fairbank, *Revolutions Within the Chinese Revolution,* 188–94.

7. Ibid., 313.
8. Thurston, *Enemies of the People*, 193–94.

NINE: Baoshan (April 1969)

1. MacFarquhar and Fairbank, *Revolutions Within the Chinese Revolution*, 196–99.
2. Ibid., 210–14.
3. Liu Binyan, review of *Lishi de yibufen* (A part of history) and *Hongse jinianbei* (Red memorial), by Zheng Yi, *New York Review of Books* 40, no. 7 (April 8, 1993): 3–6.
4. MacFarquhar and Fairbank, *Revolutions Within the Chinese Revolution*, 218–19, 262–63.
5. Ibid., 293.
6. Thurston, *Enemies of the People*, 142–44, 204.

TEN: Shanghai (February 1972)

1. MacFarquhar and Fairbank, *Revolutions Within the Chinese Revolution*, 213.
2. Ibid., 557, 572.
3. Ibid., 557, 564, 572.
4. Copy of pamphlet in author's possession, courtesy of Guan Keguang.
5. MacFarquhar and Fairbank, *Revolutions Within the Chinese Revolution*, 311–20.
6. Ibid., 320–22.
7. Ibid., 326–34.
8. Ibid., 322.
9. Ibid., 402, 404, 422.
10. Ibid., 422; and Stanley Karnow, *Mao and China* (New York: Penguin Books, 1984), 507–8.
11. Karnow, *Mao and China*, 508–9.
12. MacFarquhar and Fairbank, *Revolutions Within the Chinese Revolution*, 423.
13. Ibid., 340–41.
14. Ibid., 574.

15. Ibid.

16. Ibid; and Merle Goldman, *China's Intellectuals* (Cambridge, Mass.: Harvard University Press, 1981), 165.

17. David Bonavia, *Verdict in Peking* (New York: G. P. Putnam's Sons, 1984), 144–45.

18. Ross Terrill, *The White-Boned Demon* (New York: William Morrow, 1984), 326–27.

19. MacFarquhar and Fairbank, *Revolutions Within the Chinese Revolution*, 349.

20. Goldman, *China's Intellectuals*, 191–92.

21. Ibid., 201–13.

22. MacFarquhar and Fairbank, *Revolutions Within the Chinese Revolution*, 356.

23. Ibid., 358–65; and Thurston, *Enemies of the People*, 3–27.

24. Ibid.

25. MacFarquhar and Fairbank, *Revolutions Within the Chinese Revolution*, 365–67.

Index

121; and poster campaign, 75;
and propaganda teams, 100–
101, 102, 110; and Red Guard
membership, 72, 87. *See also*
Intellectuals
College entrance examinations,
58, 142, 151
Colleges and universities. *See*
Education; Intellectuals;
Shanghai Foreign Languages
Institute
Communications, Ministry of, 27
Communist party: Chiang's
betrayal of, 31, 33–34; as
Cultural Revolution target, 87,
101, 110, 121–22; educational
reorganization by, 57–58, 62–
63; and Hundred Flowers
movement, 60–61; and May
Fourth movement, 24; and
May Seventh Cadre Schools,
141–42; Ninth Party Congress,
121, 147; overseas Chinese
attitudes toward, 56–57;
power of, at Shanghai Foreign
Languages Institute, 64, 74;
and return of exiled
intellectuals, 53; torture
methods of, 91–92; victory of,
54–55
Confessions, 91–92, 110, 113,
131–33. *See also* Self-criticism;
Struggle sessions
Criticism sessions. *See* Struggle
sessions
Criticisms, 75–76. *See also* Self-
criticism; Struggle sessions
Cultural Revolution: and Anti-
Rightist campaign, 61; effects

of, 101–2, 121–22; end of,
121, 156; initiation of, 70–73;
library closings during, 144–
45; and May Fourth
movement, 24; party officials
as targets of, 87, 101, 110,
121–22; purpose of struggle
sessions in, 103–4; reversal of
verdicts of, 152; suicides
during, 76–77, 95–96, 108,
118; use of self-criticism
during, 92. *See also* "Monster-
beating Assembly"; Poster
campaigns; Propaganda teams;
Red Guards

Deng Xiaoping, 73, 154–56
Ding (propaganda team
member), 129

Education: American
discrimination against Chinese
in, 12, 13; Communist party
reorganization of, 57–58, 62–
63; as Cultural Revolution
issue, 71–72; post-Revolution
reforms in, 24–25; Zhou
Enlai's views on, 150–51. *See
also* Intellectuals
Eisenhower, Dwight D., 148

Fang Zhong, 70, 74–75, 80, 83,
138; betrayal of Wen by, 140–
41; at Wen's retirement, 153
First Teacher's College, 58–59
Four modernizations, 154
Four olds, 86, 87
French Concession (Shanghai), 33
Friendship Village, 63

Index

Gang of Four, 151–52, 154–56
Great Leap Forward, 62, 63
Great Proletarian Cultural Revolution. *See* Cultural Revolution
Gu (propaganda team member), 132, 133–34
Guan Keguang, 126–31, 143; confession of, 131–33; release of, 133–34
Guangxi Province: Cultural Revolution in, 122; Japanese invasion of, 50–51; Miao in, 46
Guardian, 143

Hitler, Adolf, 85
Hmong. *See* Miao tribe
Hong Kong: history of, 35; Japanese invasion of, 39–41
Hong Kong University, 55
Hou Weirui, 74–75, 94, 110, 143
Hoyt, Jake, 15
Hundred Flowers movement, 59–61, 62

Immigration: of Chinese to the United States, 13–14; to Hong Kong, 35
Intellectuals: and Hundred Flowers movement, 60–61; influence of, 25; and propaganda teams, 100–101, 102; reeducation of, 91–92, 109–10, 122–25, 141–42; and Soviet model education, 58; and two-track educational system, 62–63; Zhou Enlai's attitude toward, 53, 150–51

Japan: invasion by, 34, 38–41, 43–44, 50–51; and Treaty of Versailles, 23, 24
Jiang Qing, 102, 121, 151–52, 156
Jiang Zejiu, 109, 111
Jin Xinshu, 152, 157
Jin Yunpeng, 27

Keypoint schools, 62–63
Khrushchev, Nikita, 60, 148
Kissinger, Henry, 148
Kuo Chen. *See* Chen, Daniel

Lao Hsu, 137
Lao Lu, 137
Lei Shinan, 8
Li Guanyi, 111
Lin Biao, 73, 110, 121, 147
Lingnan University, 55
Liu Shaoqi, 62, 72, 73, 110, 154
Long Feng brothel, 10
Long March of 1934–35, 86
Lu Guangdan, 74–75, 83, 110

Manchuria, Japanese in, 34
Mao Zedong, 4, 34, 79, 109–10; and civil defense, 122; death of, 156; and Gang of Four, 151–52, 155; and Hundred Flowers movement, 60, 62; initiates Cultural Revolution, 70–71, 72, 73; and Lin Biao, 147; and May Fourth movement, 24; and May Seventh Cadre Schools, 141; and Nixon's visit, 148, 149; and Red Guards, 85, 87, 102
Mao's works, 75, 78, 86, 92, 111,

Index

Index